Profiles In Fashion
Kate Spade

Profiles In Fashion
Kate Spade

By Margo Freistadt

MORGAN REYNOLDS
PUBLISHING

Greensboro, North Carolina

Profiles in Fashion

Profiles in Fashion: Kate Spade

Library of Congress Cataloging-in-Publication Data

Freistadt, Margo.
Kate Spade / by Margo Freistadt.
    p. cm. -- (Profiles in fashion)
Includes bibliographical references and index.
ISBN 978-1-59935-154-4 (alk. paper)
1. Spade, Kate--Juvenile literature. 2. Women fashion designers--New
York (State)--New York--Biography--Juvenile literature. 3.
Handbags--Juvenile literature. I. Title.
TT505.S675.F75 2011
746.9'2092--dc22
                                        2010022227

Printed in the United States of America
First Edition

Designed by:
Ed Morgan, navyblue design studio
Greensboro, NC

For Kenny,
my thrift-store fashion whiz kid

Contents

Handbag by Kate Spade

1

You Never Grow Out of a Purse

Before Kate Spade transformed the fashion accessories market, most women's handbags were "a tedious landscape of brown and black leather," one observer noted, "light years away from the kaleidoscopic smackdown it has become." Although she prefers simple shapes and is influenced by classic designs, Kate brought a fresh, lively eye to the traditional, and changed the style of handbags women all over the world carry.

The future Kate Spade was born Katherine Noel Brosnahan in Kansas City, Missouri, in 1962. She was the fifth of six children—five girls and one boy—in an Irish Catholic family. Her mother was a full-time homemaker, and her father worked in construction, building bridges and roads. She says her sense of style developed "figuring out a way to look different from my four sisters, which was quite a challenge."

One way to dress differently was to get her mother to drive her to a local vintage shop called "Past Times." Kate was drawn to the simple, classic styles of earlier decades. "My mother thought it was great," she remembers, "because a lot of what I was buying were like things she used to wear in the

1950s and 1960s." Already with her as a child was the hunt for a look of her own, and the drive to create it by putting a new twist on something classic.

"Even when I was in my teens, I wasn't into fads," Kate recalls. "I've pretty much looked and dressed the same way for years, from my hair to my shoes (except the years 1974 to 1977, when I had the most embarrassing haircut)." Besides, growing up in Kansas City didn't expose her to trendy fashions, which left her free to develop her own taste. "When I was a kid," she says, "I didn't even know Chanel. I would have called it Channel."

From the beginning Kate liked accessories. "My mother used to let me go through her jewelry drawers. I was always drawn to her antique pieces. She would tell me little stories about whom they had belonged to and where they had come from. I think my mother loved the fact that I had an appreciation for these things."

Kate remembers learning an early lesson about accessories from a raspberry-pink velvet dress-and-purse ensemble. The dress didn't fit her, so her mother gave it to one of her sisters. Kate got the matching purse. And she thought, "You never grow out of a purse." She also loved rifling through her mother's handbag collection. "She had clutches, oranges, pinks, chocolates, huge pearl buttons," she remembers. The list brings to mind the strong, saturated colors and whimsical accents of the handbags Kate would later design.

A young Kate would often shop in vintage stores for clothing to define her own style.

Kate's father was in business for himself so entrepreneurship was part of her upbringing. She started her first business at age twelve when she and a friend organized a "camp" for the younger kids in her neighborhood. "They brought their lunch," she remembers, "but we supplied the Kool-Aid, the cookies, and of course the entertainment."

The sisters all went to Catholic school. "My mother thought we needed some religious input. I had to learn how to be proper," she remembers. "My sisters and I had to go." It was part of growing up right, being polite, not cussing. "Even now," she says many years later, "when I cuss, my mother says, 'Oh, please don't talk like this, it's sooooo vulgar.' But I'm like, 'How else am I going to tell this story?'"

Kate graduated from St. Teresa's Academy, where the high school's colors were gold, white and black—very similar to the yellow, white, and black combination that recurs frequently in Kate's designs. St. Teresa's, an academically challenging all-girls school, was founded almost 150 years ago by the Sisters of St. Joseph of Carondelet. The school touts its single-sex environment as a way to enhance "leadership, self-confidence, and the development of a positive self-image for women."

After high school, Kate enrolled at the University of Kansas. She transferred later, with her friend Elyce Arons, to Arizona State University.

At Arizona State, Kate enrolled in the journalism department. She was interested in working in television but not as an on-camera personality. "I wanted to be behind the scenes, like in that movie 'Broadcast News,'" she says. In the 1980s movie, Holly Hunter plays a hard-charging, serious-as-a-train-wreck network news producer. "Holly Hunter—her I wanted to be."

Kate had to work her way through college, so she got a job as a salesperson at a traditional men's wear store in Phoenix. "I loved fashion, I really did," she says. "But I was not obsessed with it." Her style was still her own. She didn't follow the latest trends. She still wore vintage clothing and created her own look.

Actor David Spade

Whatever direction her fashion sense was pushing her at the time, the job in the men's wear story would change Kate Brosnahan's life in another way. Also working at the store was Andy Spade, another Arizona State student who loved clothes and fashion. His brother, the actor David Spade, remembers a time when he was in eighth grade. David was getting ready for a school dance, dressed in light-blue corduroy pants and a light-blue alligator shirt. Andy stopped him, David recalls, saying, "'You can't wear that, it doesn't match.' I said, 'You idiot—it's light blue and light blue; there isn't a better match in the world.' As I walked out I heard over my shoulder, 'At least break it up with a belt.'"

Andy Spade grew up in Birmingham, Michigan, and Scottsdale, Arizona. "I was a skateboarder and outside the mainstream. At school I wasn't involved in all the stuff that the other kids were. I always wanted to do something else. My parents encouraged it: Don't think about being a doctor or a lawyer. Just use your creative skills to build something," he remembers.

When Kate met him, Andy drove an old BMW, which had a habit of breaking down. Kate sometimes drove him home after work and they became friends first and then began dating. "It was love at first sight," Andy says. "But neither one of us said anything about it. We were great friends and let it build slowly."

While he was still a student at Arizona State, Andy started an advertising agency with a friend. "In 1986," Andy says, "we were named one of the top 50 new businesses in Arizona by *Phoenix Magazine.*" He adds, with a laugh, that it must have been "a bad year for business in Arizona."

Kate graduated in 1985 from Arizona State University with her degree in broadcast journalism.

After graduation Kate, Andy and their friend Elyce Arons planned to take a low-budget, backpacking trip around Europe. But when the time came, Kate says, "Andy stayed in Arizona because of his business, and Elyce moved to New York to get going on her résumé."

Kate went to Europe alone. When she returned to the United States Kate stopped in New York to visit with Elyce. She had only seven dollars, not enough to make it back to Arizona or Kansas City. She went looking for temporary work. A temp agency sent her to *Mademoiselle* magazine, and what began as a temporary job soon turned into steady employment. Among her first tasks were fetching coffee, steam-ironing clothes for photo shoots, and running errands for the photographers. At one point her job as an assistant on a photo shoot meant she drove around Baja, Mexico, to find the one candy bar that a picky editor wanted. She asked over and over: "Yo quiero Snickers bar" ("I want a Snickers bar").

Kate found a place to live in New York, sharing a two-bedroom apartment with four other women in the decidedly unglamorous Hell's Kitchen neighborhood in Manhattan.

Kate advanced rapidly through the ranks during her five-year stint at *Mademoiselle.* By the time she was twenty-eight, she had become the senior fashion editor in charge of accessories. The pay wasn't high, but she was young and excited to be in New York and was able to get by on little. She and her older sister did try out some of Manhattan's famous restaurants, such as 21 and Elaine's. They usually shared entrées, because their budgets were so tight.

Cool young people in Manhattan at the time often wore all black, but that wasn't Kate's style. Instead, she wore lots of color. "I love, love, love green," she says. She considers it a neutral color. Her love for pink endured as well.

While she worked in New York, Andy stayed in Arizona and worked at his advertising agency. But when his partner decided to go back to Los Angeles and left him alone in the business, he decided New York might be a good alternative. "Kate had just landed this great job, and I was stuck in Arizona. So I sold the agency to someone I was working with and got on a plane and came to New York without a job." He found a job relatively quickly at the New York advertising agency Bozell & Jacobs. Soon Kate and Andy were sharing a tiny studio apartment.

Hell's Kitchen is located in New York's midtown on
the west side of Manhattan.

Kate Spade reacts during an interview in New York, 2004.

2

How
Hard
Can It Be?

After Kate had been working for five years at *Mademoiselle* magazine, she and Andy started talking about opening a business. In a lot of ways, they were successful young professionals. Kate was the assistant fashion editor in charge of accessories at a prestigious national magazine, and Andy by that time had moved to the high-powered New York advertising agency TBWA/Chiat/Day. But they were still working for other people and Kate's salary was uninspiring. She was making $14,500 a year, not a high salary in Manhattan in 1992. Andy explains, "We've seen the people on television and in the newspapers who were laid off when they were 50 years old. We both knew what it was like to struggle, to have to work our way through school. Kate had just seven dollars when she first got to New York City. We didn't want to go through all that anymore. We wanted to chase our own destiny."

Surprisingly, Kate said later about their plans that "It was less about wanting to be a designer and more wanting to start a business."

As they told the story years later to Jackie White of the Knight-Ridder News Service, they were dining in a Mexican restaurant on the Upper West Side of Manhattan. Kate said she'd like to start her own business. Me too, Andy said.

He asked: "What would you like to do?"

Kate didn't have a ready answer. So Andy made a suggestion. "You can never find a handbag you like. Why don't you do handbags?"

When she said, "I don't know much about making bags," Andy asked, "How hard can it be?"

So, with more optimism than planning, Kate and Andy launched a company.

Andy was right. Kate never could find a handbag she liked. Sure, high-end department stores offered luxury European handbags made by Gucci, Prada, and Armani, but she found them to be plain and unappealing. The bag she carried was, as often as not, something makeshift, such as a wicker bag without a flap or zipper. "It was rectangular and completely open," she says. "I'd take a scarf in the winter to cover the top in case it snowed."

Kate recalls: "There was a lot of retro-looking, cutesy-ish lady stuff out there at the time." Her objections to those high-end designer bags were two-fold. They weren't practical or fun.

"Many fashion people make these teeny-tiny bags for this small group of customers. It's all just about saying to everyone else in the design community, 'Hey, look what I can do,'" she says. "But what I kept seeing in my head was larger—a square or a rectangle—and it was strong-looking, almost like a suitcase. It wasn't precious, it didn't have a lot of hardware, maybe it was nylon or straw, but higher quality than something you'd buy on the beach in Mexico. Somewhere between L.L. Bean and Prada—preppy, but more artful than the Ralph Lauren blue blazer kind of look. More John Kennedy than Prince Charles. It was bag I wanted to own, and I couldn't find it anywhere."

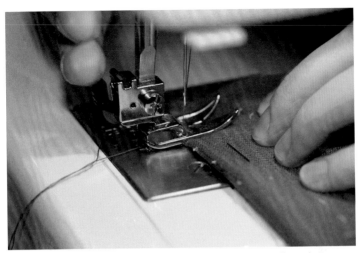

Kate and Andy knew that finding sewing and manufacturing
plants were important steps at the beginning of the business.

Kate set out to make bags that she wanted to own. She was
an expert on accessories by then, including handbags, from
her work at *Mademoiselle.* But she didn't know the first thing
about manufacturing, or how to design a bag, or sew one, or
market or sell anything.

"I didn't have any idea what to do at all," she recalls. "I
didn't have the slightest clue about where to get fabric, how
to make patterns, or who would make the labels and sell me
the zippers."

Because Andy made more money than Kate, they decided
she would quit her job to work on the business. Andy would
keep his job at the advertising agency so they could cover
their rent and other expenses. This also would give them
some income to pump into the business. It was a cautious
way to begin. A more risky move would have been to borrow
"start-up money" and pay it back from the proceeds of the business—assuming it's successful. If it wasn't they would have
to pay the money back themselves.

Kate's first bag was made of burlap and raffia.

Kate and Andy weren't comfortable with debt. "To have borrowed even $1,000 would have made it too hard for both of us to sleep at night, especially since we weren't sure the business was going to make it," Kate says. "We didn't mind losing our own money, but losing someone else's would have been the worst."

Another precaution: Kate didn't burn her bridges at the magazine. "When I left *Mademoiselle*," she said, "I asked if I could return if this failed."

While this strategy meant that their business had to grow more slowly than it might have otherwise, if it succeeded all of it would belong to them alone. To get started they both cashed out their retirement savings, about $6,000 total, to fund the start-up.

During the first years of their business their situation was financially insecure. Andy recalls, "Our friends were buying their first homes. They had money in the stock market. We didn't know for sure that the business was going to work."

The first order of business was to make a distinctive handbag—one that would stand out enough that women would just have to buy it. In their tiny apartment, Kate recalls, "I sat down with some tracing paper, and I knew immediately what the shape should be—a very simple square." She cut and pasted paper until she got the proportions exactly the way she wanted. She was looking for strong, basic shapes, in sizes large enough to be practical. "At the time no one was doing anything that clean. The shape gave me a real flexible canvas for applying all the ideas I had for a lot of colors, patterns, and fabrics."

Kate made several prototypes out of construction paper and tape. The first handbag was made of burlap, with a decorative fringe of raffia. "I neurosed over every single second of it," she says. She wanted a simple classical shape that wouldn't immediately go out of style. It should be a relatively large size, big enough to be practical for real women carrying all the day-to-day stuff. But she also wanted some whimsical decoration that could add a bit of fun. "Handbags should be both," she says. "That's what designers were forgetting. So many bags can hold the kitchen sink but they're just big black bags."

From the beginning, her handbags were definitely not "just big black bags." Later, Suzanne C. Ryan of the *Boston Globe* admiringly described them: "Picture a square straw purse with large colorful flowers woven into it. Or a silk tote adorned with bright pink and red alternating stripes. How about a red silk-satin evening clutch?" The purses that got the attention were the colorful ones, of course, but the basis of her collection, from the outset, was a simple square-ish black totebag in satin-finish nylon.

After Kate had designed her bags, the next step was to have samples made that she could take to trade shows. She was nervous about using her contacts from when she worked at *Mademoiselle*. "Since I had seen so many collections in advance," she says. "I thought people would be afraid I'd copy them." So she did what people did in the days before the Internet when exploring an area they knew nothing about. She went to the Yellow Pages of the phone book and looked up "sewing." That didn't help.

"I tried a lot of things that didn't work," she recalls, while looking for someone to manufacture samples of her designs. "I rang doorbells in Chinatown in New York, where a lot of the garment factories are." Then someone told her to look at ads in the back of *Women's Wear Daily*, the trade magazine for the New York garment industry, for handbag pattern-makers. "They make

Mott Street, the unofficial Main Street of Chinatown in
New York City, is home to many garment factories.

Kate Spade

a technical pattern," she explains, "and then they make a sample."

Since the business had no track record, Kate had a hard time finding business people who would work with her. "Once I started going to these factories and fabric companies, though, most people wouldn't take me seriously. One guy told me later that he didn't think I would pay because I had a hole in my sweater. I think a lot of students come in planning to manufacture things but never go through with it."

Another time, "One [fabric supplier] said to me, 'Honey, you look like a nice girl. You don't want to get into the business. Settle down.'" Finally someone gave her the name of a business in Brooklyn that agreed to work with her.

Andy and Kate still didn't have a name for their company. This was important for a host of reasons, but just for starters, they had to get labels made. Kate toyed with different names. "Olive" and "Alex Noel" were under consideration. "I loved Olive for some reason," she recalls.

While they were visiting friends in Provincetown, on the tip of Massachusetts's Cape Cod, Kate finally agreed to Andy's suggestion that they combine her first name, Kate, and his last name, Spade. "Andy kept saying 'Kate Spade. Kate Spade,'" she says. And he won her over. "Kate Spade wasn't frilly. It was just straightforward. It wasn't a fashion-y name." It was the feel they were aiming for. So it was that Kate Spade was Kate Brosnahan's company name three years before it was her name. By the time Kate and Andy married in 1995, the "Kate Spade" name was on thousands of purses.

Back in Kansas City, in 1992, Kate's Catholic mother lacked faith that the two of them would take that next step. When Kate told her of their choice for a company name her mother said, "He'll never marry you now!"

Kate and Andy Spade in New York, 2007

Kate Spade during an interview in New York, 2004

3

It Didn't Cover the Cost of the Show

As much as Kate and Andy liked the bags she had designed, they would only make money if they could get them in stores. Boutiques and department stores have buyers whose job is to select and buy stock for their stores. The most efficient way to see a lot of buyers at one time is to sign up for "trade shows," which are conventions where a lot of sellers and buyers in a given industry meet. Manufacturers set up booths to show their latest work and buyers look around and order products that they think will sell in their stores. Trade shows exist for all sorts of products: cars, electronic gear, toys, and agriculture to name a few. Handbag buyers and sellers meet at "accessories trade shows."

The year after starting their business, Andy and Kate had six sample handbag designs ready. They thought it was time to take them to an accessories trade show. Since they were living in New York City, they could take their Kate Spade bags to the big 1993 accessories show at Javits Center, the enormous convention center on Eleventh Avenue on the west side of midtown Manhattan.

They didn't get a great spot at the trade show. When they signed up the only spot they could get was way in the back of the convention center, near the hot dog stand. Andy recalls: "The people with seniority get the better space, even though you don't pay less for bad space." Even as the young entrepreneurs stepped up to the big time to show their work to accessories buyers from all over the country, they tried to stay within a budget as well as stay true to their own style. Rather than use slick, commercial display racks and tables, they used their wiles to create an off-beat vintage look for their booth. Andy remembers: "We moved in furniture from our apartment because we didn't like commercial displays and because it was cheaper."

The night before the trade show, Kate was still not sure the bags were ready. She recalls: "There was something missing. We needed something for the eye to go to." So she stayed up all night pulling out the stitching that had attached the little black-and-white "Kate Spade New York" labels to the inside of the handbags. She then reattached them to the outside of the bags. "You can imagine pushing through all that cardboard with a needle," she says.

The simple small label stitched on the outside gave the Kate Spade bags a distinctive look. In addition, "kate spade"— spelled out in lower case letters on the label—created the beginning of a recognizable brand.

Kate's fingers were puffy and sore the next day, and she and her bags were in the most out-of-the-way place possible in the enormous convention hall. But they got five hundred dollars in orders—and the orders were from Barneys and Charivari, two high-fashion, trend-setting stores in Manhattan.

"It was thrilling, she remembered later." Kate said in several articles that she was ready to give up at that point, she was really not thrilled. So it would be more accurate if that said: Despite getting those orders, Kate was disappointed: "It didn't cover the cost of the show."

Despite the discouraging balance sheet, having Kate Spade bags in Barneys and Charivari was important. It announced to the fashion world that the bags were worth being noticed.

The distinctive Kate Spade logo on one of her signature
basic square bags

Also, Kate and Andy's display at the Javits Center had caught the eye of some fashion magazine editors. Kate's bags were included in an accessories column in *Vogue* a few months later. "We were on the same page with Chanel, Prada, and Gucci," Kate says. "I was like, 'I'm going to faint!'"

Having an off-beat-looking booth in the far-back of the trade show might not have been such a bad thing, Andy says in retrospect. "The great thing is, the fashion editors who can break a product like ours out are like people in flea markets; they're always looking around in corners for the next great find. And that's how the woman from Barneys found us."

The first six bags Kate displayed included the simple square-ish black satin-finish nylon bag that became an icon for her company. With few changes it stayed in her collection for years—the physical manifestation of her idea that a classic piece will stay in style and keep looking good for many years.

In the fashion world, the price point is a key consideration. At the time, leather Gucci bags were priced at four hundred dollars to $1,000 and Prada bags started at around $350. A bag from J. C. Penny's might have cost twenty dollars. Kate's bags were priced between the two ends of the scale, starting from around sixty to one hundred dollars. This is called the "bridge" market. Her handbags were less expensive than the very high-end bags, but more fashionable, more fun, and carrying more status than a non-name-brand bag. She was able to keep the costs down by using fabrics like nylon rather than leather, and her unique, recognizable designs and quality workmanship made the bags desirable.

Kate's handbags stood out both in style and philosophy. Several years later, a glowing newspaper report said: "Spade, whose philosophy is 'bags should assume the personality of the wearer, not the reverse,' specializes in classic shapes (totes and clutches mostly) modernized with fashionable colors (including pink, red, and black) and materials (silk, canvas, nylon) . . . And women love them."

Actress/singer Nona Gaye, daughter of soul legend Marvin Gaye, carries a basic Kate Spade handbag.

Kate's handbags sold well once they got into the right stores. Kate says, "They sold quickly. We got some reorders, and it was time to show another collection. Then we were showing five markets a year, which means doing designs five times a year. I kept showing the same square shapes." She soon ran into resistance from buyers, who were more accustomed to designers always pushing something new, something that would be fashionable for only one season.

Of that particular struggle, Kate says, "I remember Barneys saying, 'Yup, you showed us those shapes last time. It's just new fabric.' And I said, 'Well, that's the idea. That's the concept.'" She didn't want a totally new look every season. She wanted looks that women would wear year after year.

Andy describes it this way: "We wanted to create the next Levi's 501 jeans, L.L. Bean shoes—one of those items that continue forever. I love that one shoe that Converse makes—the Jack Purcell. They're just great icons. That's why we continued with the shape. The collection was very tight, very edited, for the first two years. I think if we had changed the shape, our bags would have gotten lost. But we had to insist. Then fortunately the consumer started responding, and the stores kept reordering. So it worked. And that made us identifiable."

However, before any of that could happen, Kate had to figure out how to manufacture the bags at a cost low enough to allow them to make a profit. Just as she had learned about technical patterns and samples on the fly, she had to start from scratch in figuring out the manufacturing of quantities larger than the samples she had made originally. Again, she talked to people, looked in the Yellow Pages and used the library at New York's Fashion Institute of Technology. She found out very quickly that the main problem at the beginning was she was making too few bags for any real producer to be interested. Manufacturers wanted big orders for thousands of bags. Also, wholesale fabric companies had large minimum orders because it's not profitable for them to sell small amounts.

"Most people won't sell you less than 1,000 yards of fabric per color," Kate says. "But bags don't use that much fabric, and we were just starting, so there was no way we could use that much." However, fabric companies give out "sample yardage" to designers, so they can make prototypes for shows. The fabric company hopes that when orders are made from the prototype, the manufacturer will order that fabric when production starts. Kate's production run was so small that she managed, in some cases, to get enough fabric in "sample yardage" do her whole production run.

Kate did finally find some smaller suppliers that would work with her. Andy explained: "When you show buyers a bag in a particular fabric, you need to know stock is available. So Kate went to the Yellow Pages and located a company that made potato sacks. She called up and found out that they had no minimum order size. So we bought burlap from the potato sack company and sewed bags out of it."

Another way to work around the fabric problem was to share orders with other designers. Young designers cooperating, rather than competing in a cut-throat way, was so unusual that her willingness to do so brought Kate attention. *New York Times* reporter Constance C. R. White wrote a column in June of 1995 that mentioned that "Kate Spade's trendy handbags and Susan Lazar's up-to-the-minute nylon trench coats were cut from the same fabric because the designers combined their fabric purchases." White commented further: "Designers in the under-40 set are displaying esprit de corps not widely seen before, sharing advice on everything from real estate to stores' payment habits. They are pooling information, socializing and even turning up at each other's runway shows."

White quoted Cynthia Rowley, a young designer (also from the Midwest) whose gown Kate wore at her wedding, on why young designers were turning to each other for help: "'Designers used to think they could get the big backer who would put them on easy street,' Ms. Rowley said. 'That's just not the case anymore.'"

The Spades' business grew quickly once high-end stores such as Barneys began selling Kate's bags.

Like Kate and Andy Spade, other young designers at the time were figuring out ways to build their businesses without borrowing a huge amount of money upfront. Many leased space in the relatively inexpensive SoHo section of New York, the neighborhood Kate and Andy settled on when their business outgrew their tiny apartment.

Even with their ingenious solutions for getting small quantities of fabrics, Kate and Andy still needed webbing for the bags' handles. And webbing had to be bought in bulk. That, Andy says, "was a decision that paralyzed Kate."

It was a huge purchase for them at the time. "It was going to cost us $1,500," Kate says. "Andy was taking a shower, and . . . I was thinking, 'Let's back out before we get in over our heads.'" But they persevered and the orders for the bags kept coming in. Soon other large, well-known New York department stores like Neiman Marcus, Saks Fifth Avenue, Nordstrom, and Bloomingdale's were carrying Kate Spade bags.

These are large chains, with the ability to send handbags to hundreds of stores across the country. The production started to stretch the limits of what Kate and Andy could accommodate in their apartment. During shipping season, they had to stay with friends because the apartment was stacked full of handbags.

Life wasn't all work. At one point Kate decided it was time to have a real grown-up dinner party. Kate remembers that Andy "was all for it, but he also knew that, considering this would be my first dinner party, a little warning was in order." So he made copies of instructions for the Heimlich maneuver, the emergency measure for people who are choking on their food. The instructions, in poster form, went out to their friends, Andy says, "sealed with a sticker containing the words 'You are invited to Kate's first dinner party.' "

In late 1993, Kate and Andy brought their friend Pamela Bell into the business to help with all the production details, such as locating supplies, finding contractors, and shipping inventory.

And the next year, Elyce Arons, their old friend from college, joined the company to help with sales and public relations. Both Pamela and Elyce joined as "sweat equity" investors. Rather than investing money, like traditional investors, their investment was hard work. Their sweat earned them a share in the ownership of the company, called equity. For Kate and Andy, that meant giving up part of the ownership in exchange for help. As Kate put it later: "The question is, do you want 100 percent of nothing or some smaller part of something?" As it turned out, it was a smaller part of something much, much bigger. As for the "sweat equity" partners, Pamela and Elyce, they worked for the first several years for little or no salary, as did Kate and Andy.

About three years into their business partnership, Kate and Andy married. Kate Brosnahan became Kate Spade. Now her name matched her label. The couple threw two parties for the wedding, so Kate had two gowns—one by Isaac Mizrahi and another, with a long silver skirt, by Cythnia Rowley. "The flowers were great, the music was just right, and Kate's dress was amazing," Andy remembers. "Kate has a thing about candles, especially votives, so she had them strategically placed around the house, even along the staircase. Kate made her arrival coming down the stairs, but there was one problem—the votives caught the train of her wedding dress and set it on fire."

Kate put out the fire, and burst out laughing.

"Whatever notions either of us had about the day being precious," Andy added, "went out the window."

Kate Spade attends the Chanel Tribeca Film Festival
Dinner in New York, 2006.

4

Huge Growth We Didn't Expect

O ver the next years, after their marriage, the company grew rapidly. Kate and Andy didn't have formal or academic business training, so they felt their way along, learning as they went. This meant they did many things differently from other companies, sometimes as intentional choices, and sometimes by accident.

In 1995, Kate Spade served as her own model in the company's first advertising campaign. This started a long narrative in which Kate's own life was intertwined with her products. It became a signature of their advertising and public relations. She was a perfect fit for the product—dark-haired, with Irish American wholesome good looks, and a ready laugh. One writer said her image was "as if Audrey Hepburn had been raised in Kansas City." Most important, she is not intimidating—not frighteningly slender or model-tall. Quite the contrary. Kate is five-foot-two, "fun-sized," she calls it. (Andy is five-foot-five.) Her hair's signature look is an up-do that she arranges herself with bobby pins. She wears timeless clothes, not this year's fashions. "I look back at pictures of all of us from college," Elyce says, "and there's me in some goofball trendy outfit, and there's Kate in the perfect navy peacoat, the perfect fisherman's sweater. . . .The thing is, back then I used to think that I was the fashionable one."

In 1995 Kate appeared in one of the company's first advertising posters on walls all over Manhattan and Los Angeles. She was posed in a '50s-style kitchen. It was an image that reminded people of someone they knew, or perhaps even of themselves.

The Council of Fashion Designers of American took note of Kate's bags in late 1995 and honored her with the Perry Ellis Award for Accessory Design, a prestigious award presented to new designers. At the black-tie awards ceremony at Lincoln Center in Manhattan she was on the same program with established superstars of the fashion world like Ralph Lauren, who was designer of the year for women's wear, and Tommy Hilfiger, who won for men's wear. Kate's contribution to the festivities was described as "the evening's most entertaining video—two girls drag racing through suburbia to reach a Kate Spade handbag first."

Kate's first big award signaled that the fashion world was noticing her designs, and that retailers should take her seriously. In the next months, her bags started selling at department stores across the country. In March 1996, a writer in the *Chicago Tribune* remarked that until recently, Kate Spade bags were known only to a small circle of upscale East Coast trendsetters, but had begun to adorn the arms of fashion-forward women all over the country. The writer took note, as so many people did, of the easy-to-love classic shapes and the whimsical fabrics and patterns like peacoat wool, Novasuede, linen, Harris tweed, herringbone, and potato-sack burlap.

After she won the Perry Ellis award, *People* magazine reported that her bags were being snapped up by celebrities such as Cindy Crawford, Mary Tyler Moore, and Sandra Bullock. "I never bought anything more than huge trash bags for all my junk," *People* quoted Bullock, the famous

Sandra Bullock at the 2005 Teen Choice awards

American actress. "Then I walked into Kate's showroom and discovered I now have an obsession." The bags' bright colors, like the orange nylon messenger bag and pink imitation suede bag that *People* cited, brought in legions of followers. At the same time, Kate stayed true to her design lodestar by keeping classic shapes and the idea that a handbag should last many seasons, not just one: "If you can't keep wearing the things in our line," she told *People*, "then we feel we made a mistake."

By late 1996, just three years after she launched the company, Kate was one of eight designers surveyed when *Women's Wear Daily* wanted a peek at what the design world could expect in handbags for the spring season. True to form, Kate pointed to classic American nostalgic inspirations: "Kate Spade says her overall direction for spring is inspired by 'upscale, suburban Connecticut lawn parties. Think elegant patio parties á la those in the movie 'High Society.' It's very

1950's suburban evenings." The article told people to expect colors like pool blues, lilac, and lawn green, "all in Spade's signature simple shapes, as well as new styles like a soft, not-too-slouchy squared hobo. Canvas and awning fabrics lend an up-to-the moment touch."

That year, the Kate Spade company opened its first free-standing boutique, a very small retail shop at Fifty-nine Thompson Street in the SoHo area of lower Manhattan, not far from their Tribeca loft. Kate and Andy hired the young architects Jonathan Marvel and Robert Rogers to design the shop. After brainstorming with Kate, they designed the space with materials that reflected back specifically on the world of handbags. They used Bontex, a material for stiffening the bottoms of bags, for wall lamination and wrapped the display shelves with Kalf-stay, a rubber material used in the linings of handbags. The tiny store was original and interesting enough to be written up in a magazine. Marvel and Rogers would work with Kate and Andy on many future projects.

Opening the boutique was a hard decision. Kate was hesitant because of the cost, but Andy believed it was time to establish freestanding Kate Spade stores. Like other married couples that work together, they had to figure out a way to resolve conflicts on the job. What they came up with was, whoever feels more strongly gets to make the decision. Andy got that one, and it was so successful that it outgrew its space in a year. Kate laughed later: "Now Andy gets to say, 'I told you so.'"

Despite the boutique's small size—four hundred square feet—the store was organized and uncluttered and carried the full line of Kate Spade handbags and totes. In this first store, Kate and Andy set in place a tradition that they would carry on in future retail ventures. Reflecting their own fascination with esoteric finds, the store included offerings other than Kate's own creations. These appeared to be almost random things that caught their fancy, such as scarves and hats, and, as one reporter said, "those Indian bead belts that were popular in the fifties."

"Besides cementing our image," Kate said at the time, "we want the store to be one of those places you find the unexpected great item." Since it was her store, she could indulge her love for thrift shop chic and the thrill of the finding a unique treasure in a flea market. It also expressed her belief that inspiration can be found anywhere, often in objects from earlier eras.

SoHo at the time was making a transition from being an area of artists' lofts and art galleries to a district that also includes boutiques and other shops. Kate Spade was among its first boutique fashion shops. By the next year, many other designers and clothing companies—including Gucci, Ralph Lauren, and Old Navy—were perusing the area for retail space.

In addition to sales at trade shows and her own shop, Kate's bags were offered at the Cynthia O'Connor showroom. It was a "trade only" outlet, where wholesale buyers could purchase Kate's designs on a regular basis, not just at trade shows. By the end of 1996, the sales of Kate Spade handbags totaled almost $10 million dollars for the year. The business would double the following year.

Andy finally quit his day job as senior vice president and creative director of the advertising agency TBWA/Chiat/Day and went to work full-time with their company. He took the title of president and creative director of Kate Spade. For the past three years, he'd been essentially working two jobs—at the advertising agency on weekdays and on the Kate Spade business during evenings and weekends.

Andy's step was a big enough deal to be reported in trade publications for both their industries. "Andy Spade Becomes President of Kate Spade Handbags" was the headline in *AdWeek* and *Women's Wear Daily*, sometimes called the "Bible" of the fashion industry, reported: "Spade Times Two— accessories designer Kate Spade, her husband, Andy, to join her firm."

A freestanding Kate Spade store in the Flatiron Building in Manhattan

Andy remembers:

I decided to quit my job to join Kate in 1996 because we were turning into a real business, which was challenging. When you start your own company, you get to be creative, but at the same time you're responsible for running a company. Nobody tells you that. . . . . In advertising I was working only with creative people. In this company, you're dealing with payroll, accounting, and shipping and warehouses, which I'd never dealt with and which I'd never wanted to deal with. We started to think, 'How do we do this thing well without putting ourselves under? The business experienced this huge growth we didn't expect. When the CEOs from the big stores told us how much they'd sold that week, it would scare both of us. We would say, 'Can you honestly slow down? You have to make sure the presentation is right.' The CEOs were shocked.

Even as the business grew dramatically, Kate, Andy, Pamela, and Elyce tried to keep the brand's feel of a small boutique so that their handbags would seem unique and personal to the buyer. They gave their products names such as "Sonia," for her popular satin-finish nylon bag. When they started a line of stationery, they named one of the first products "Molly," after one of Kate's sisters. They wanted the Kate Spade line to reflect a specific look, a specific attitude.

Kate got a reputation of going to Kate Spade displays in stores and straightening up the shelves to make sure that everything was tidy and displayed just so. Sometimes department store clerks mistook her for an obsessive-compulsive shopper who couldn't stand to look at purses that were not lined up perfectly. "It's instinct," she says. "I feel good as long as the products are merchandised well. If they're not, I just start rearranging things myself. I tell retailers not to get upset if they find me doing that."

The distinctive, simple look of the Kate Spade bags, along with their growing popularity, caused another unanticipated problem—knock-offs, or counterfeits. As early as 1996 Kate and her company had to take steps to stop other companies from copying her designs. Banana Republic agreed, without going to court, to stop selling knock-offs of Kate's designs. But in January of 1997, the Kate Spade company filed a copyright infringement suit in Manhattan's federal court against Kmart and Dayton Hudson, the parent corporation of Target stores. She asked the court to require the two huge chains to stop selling copies of her purses and to destroy any knock-offs in stock. She also asked for damages and legal costs. In the suit she pointed out that the stores were selling exact replicas of her bags, even down to the small black-and-white labels— although they had a different brand name.

Kate's bags were different enough from others on the market that the court agreed. "Back in the early '90s, no one was doing square totes and no one was using fabrics such as nylon or linen," Kate says. "Today they are, but back then that's what differentiated us. . . .We were able to establish a recognizable aesthetic identity. . . . So we said, let's set a precedent, and they eventually agreed to desist."

When big companies openly sold copies of her bags, Kate could sue and force them to stop. Another development in the copycat world was much harder to control. Soon street vendors, too numerous and too elusive to sue, were selling knock-offs of her bags. Street vendors also started selling actual counterfeits,

continued on page 58

When a Spade Is Not a Spade

For many years, Kate Spade bags were "such a status object," one observer remarked, "that knockoffs were for sale on every midtown corner" in Manhattan. Many women didn't want to pay or couldn't afford the price of real bags, and wanted them badly enough to step into the gray area of buying fakes.

Counterfeits are fake designer products, such as jeans or purses, that are fraudulently sold as the designer's own work. Sometimes the products are almost identical to the real thing even down to the labels, and it's very hard to tell that they're counterfeit. Other times, items are not even similar or are very badly constructed, and the labels are poor copies, so it's easy to tell they are fakes. At times the designers' names are even misspelled.

Knock-offs are products that are not pretending to be the designer's own work, they are just similar, copying the design. Both counterfeits and knock-offs are much cheaper than the name-brand products, which is why people buy them.

Trafficking in counterfeits is a huge, illegal, multinational business. The trade includes DVDs and music, designer clothes, handbags, car parts, electronic equipment, computer software, sporting goods, shoes, even prescription medicines—any product that someone can copy and sell for less than the owner of the design, copyright, or patent. As much as 5 percent to 7 percent of global trade is in fake merchandise, valued at hundreds of billions of dollars a year, according to the International Chamber of Commerce's Counterfeiting Intelligence Bureau. The money, unregulated and untaxed, immediately enters the underground economy, and some has been traced to organized crime and funding for terrorism.

In 2003, Barbara Kolsun, general counsel for Kate Spade, estimated that for every legitimate Kate Spade bag sold, at least one counterfeit or knock-off was sold, losses worth many millions of dollars. The fake bags were sold on eBay and other Internet auction sites, by street vendors, at flea markets, from small storefront businesses, and through "purse parties" like Tupperware parties.

Most of the bags were made in China or in Latin America, and smuggled into the United States. Sometimes the labels were sewn on after the bags arrived in America, taking advantage of a loophole in the federal law that defines trade in counterfeits.

The trade in counterfeits and knock-offs carries risks and costs for everyone. The consumer risks buying badly made, unwarranted products. The buyer also has no assurance that workers who produced the items were paid a living wage and treated fairly. The designers and originators of the product don't get paid for their work. And cities, states, and countries lose billions of dollars in taxes, shortchanging funds for schools, parks, police, health care, and other services. This leaves a higher tax burden on the people and companies who play by the rules.

With the advent of the Internet, design counterfeiting got faster and bolder. Products were shown at trade shows or fashion events, and pictures could be sent by e-mail to factories in China. Knock-offs could be on the streets before the real products were in department stores. That process used to take long enough that designers at least had one clear season to sell their work before knock-offs were available.

As counterfeiting got bolder and more commonplace, Kate Spade and other brand-name designers banded together to try to fight the problem—by investigating and reporting large-scale operations to law enforcement agencies, by sending legal "cease and desist" letters to storefront businesses, and by hiring people to monitor online auction sites. It was enough of a concern that the Kate Spade company hired Kolsun in 2002 as an in-house lawyer. Her previous job had been with the International AntiCounterfeiting Coalition.

The anti-counterfeiting crusade had some successes, confiscating huge hauls of fake products. In 2004, just in New York City, police seized more than $20 million in merchandise in ten raids. But it was just a tiny slice of the action. The city controller estimated that counterfeiting cost New York City businesses $23 billion just in 2003, depriving the city of $1 billion in tax revenue—enough he said, to put a nurse in every public school, hire 12,000 police officers, and buy 10 million school books.

Selling counterfeit merchandise is a federal crime, so it's illegal in every state, with penalties of up to ten years in prison and hefty fines. In addition to that concern, Kolsun says, "People have to look at the bigger picture. It's about stealing. It's not just about handbags; it's about any consumer product–toys, drugs. Counterfeiters are criminals." She adds, "Where do people think those $20 Kate Spade knockoffs are made? They're made by children in sweatshops in China. We also manufacture in China, but we work with the best factories, which are human rights-compliant. Because that's what good companies do. All of those things go into the cost of a Kate Spade bag."

William Lash, a deputy U.S. commerce secretary, rips apart a fake Kate Spade bag during a press conference in Beijing, China, in April 2005. Calling China the source of global piracy, Lash accused Beijing of failing to take seriously the rampant counterfeiting that is costing American business billions in lost revenue.

which are copies that sellers try to pass off as the real designer product—even down to fake labels with the designer's name.

Growth created stresses on other fronts. "We were running our business out of our home, a loft in Tribeca," Andy says. "Workers would show up at six in the morning. We had so many boxes in our 1,800-square-foot loft during shipping time that we had a path from the bedroom to the bathroom." The apartment wasn't an ideal place to do business in the summertime. "It was hot," Andy remembers of a particularly bad spell. "We had no air conditioning, and it was August."

And living and working in the same place with the same partner has a whole other set of challenges, as many married couples have discovered. The business wouldn't succeed unless they put their all into it, but they didn't have a way to keep it from taking over their lives. "We had to learn how to turn off the business at home," Kate says. "Andy was better than me. I talked about it 24 hours a day. I would pop out of bed and blah, blah, blah, and go to bed, blah, blah. We started straightening that out a couple of years ago. We just said, 'This is insane. I think it's all we talk about.'"

"It was difficult," Andy remembers. "We'd wake up on the weekends and still be in the office. There was no separation." So Kate and Andy bought a place outside the city where they could unwind, even before they could afford to buy an apartment in New York. They found a fixer-upper on North Main Street in Southampton on Long Island—an 1870s farmhouse that had been a barn until a renovation in the 1920s.

Southampton is one of a cluster of small seaside resort towns on the east end of Long Island, an area called the Hamptons, about an hour and a half drive from Manhattan. The area is accessible enough—by car and train—to be a popular spot for second homes for wealthy families from New York and other population centers of the East Coast.

When they bought it the house was completely run down, from the leaking roof to the peeling wallpaper. "We fell in love with it," Andy says, "and we needed it for our mental health."

It had what Kate desired—mature trees on the property that recalled her midwestern background, especially a giant weeping beech in the front yard. And it had what Andy desired, "Proximity to the beach."

They also finally got a much larger warehouse for production and storage, so they could move as much of the business as possible out of the loft. They leased a 10,000-square-foot space on West Twenty-fifth Street. It almost quadrupled the size of their previous storage area, a small 2,800-square-foot warehouse. Their headquarters would stay on West Twenty-fifth Street for many years.

A Kate Spade store in the SoHo neighborhood of New York

5

Whatever Needs to be Done is the Job

Kate and Andy's company continued to grow rapidly. They were becoming a force in the world of fashion design.

By the late 1990s, the Kate Spade look was well established. It was intended to appeal to a woman who takes care with her appearance, dresses relatively conservatively and modestly, but also likes some fun in her clothes. Without unnecessarily drawing attention to herself, she's not afraid to add a touch of brilliant color or unusual fabric in her accessories. Gingham, denim, and faux zebra were a few of the many materials Kate played with during this time—and pink and green were never far away.

The world of fashion gave Kate the ultimate nod when the Council of Fashion Designers of America honored her as the 1997 Accessories Designer of the Year. It was just two years after she had won the Perry Ellis honor for new talent. The three top awards that year all went to relatively young designers: Kate for accessories, Marc Jacobs for women's wear, and John Bartlett for men's wear. At the ceremony, in

February 1998, Kate shared the program with *Vogue* editor Anna Wintour, an industry icon, who was receiving a special award for her Global Influence on Fashion, and legendary actress Elizabeth Taylor, who was honored for a Lifetime of Glamour. It was prestigious company for a thirty-four-year-old from Kansas City.

However, the success didn't happen on its own. Kate, Andy, Elyce, and Pamela were working hard, starting new ventures and expanding the business continuously.

In late 1997, Kate Spade produced her first leather bags. Again, she was prompted by not being able to find a bag, this time in leather, that she wanted to own.

"There wasn't one leather handbag that I really wanted to carry," she said, echoing her thoughts when she first started making handbags. She told a reporter: "We're looking to capture the same market we have with the fabric bags—simple, strong, understated and functional, but with a level of fun and style not seen in other functional bags."

The leather bags stayed true to Kate's philosophy—simpler is better. Made of black Miora Italian leather, they sported off-white stitching. Kate started with six simple shapes, including her standard rectangular and "bucket" styles. The purses had straightforward, friendly names like "Caroline," "Clair," and "Sam."

Italian leather costs a lot more than nylon, canvas, burlap, denim, or imitation suede. So the costs were higher, pushing some of her prices nearer those of the higher-end designer bags. But there was a flurry of interest from the very beginning. When she showed them at the August accessories trade show, department stores competed for orders.

Kate also started designing smaller leather goods, like wallets and other smaller accessories, that went along with the leather handbags.

The company also began producing diaper bags, recognizing that just because a woman has a baby doesn't mean she wants to carry around a bag trimmed with a row of yellow

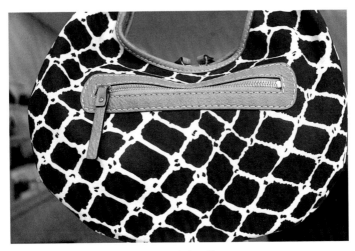

Kate Spade handbag

teddy bears. Kate slightly modified her fashion handbags and lined them with moisture-proof materials for easy clean-up.

As they expanded their offerings, Kate and Andy were still clarifying exactly where they fit in the fashion world. They started to define their company in terms of a lifestyle and an image. "We call our pieces distorted classics," Andy said at the time. "They represent an eclectic mix of things we really like. We're not trying to sell them in an edgy way either. We think our Midwestern sensibility and being charming and polite can be really cool and modern, too. It's pervasive in everything we're doing—we're not 100 percent there yet, but are moving toward that concept."

Retail sales quickly outgrew the tiny SoHo store on Thompson Street. Kate and Andy found a store twice as big at Broome and Mercer Streets in the center of SoHo. Jonathan Marvel and Robert Rogers again designed the space, using an ebony stain on the fir flooring and letting their design emphasize the beauty of the existing eighteen-foot-high ceilings. The new boutique opened in fall of 1997. Again, the magazine *Interior Design* described the store in glowing terms.

The first freestanding Kate Spade store outside of New York opened, in Tokyo, as a result of a licensing agreement with the Japanese companies Itochu Fashion System and Sanei International. The agreement meant Kate and Andy didn't have to learn all the details of running a business in Japan. They just designed the products, and Itochu and Sanei would develop several dozen stand-alone stores and in-store shops over the next few years. Marvel and Rogers worked on the look of the stores in Japan.

Meanwhile, Kate and her crew searched for the right places in the right cities for retail stores in the United States. The first to open was a 1,500-square-foot shop in Los Angeles on trendy Robertson Boulevard. The second store was on Boston's Newbury Street. They also scouted locations in Chicago, San Francisco, and Atlanta, but they were not interested in simply opening as many stores as possible. "We can't really put a number on how many stores we want," Andy said at the time. "It's all about the architecture and locations we find interesting and appropriate for our designs."

During the same time, the company introduced its first products not directly related to handbags—stationery and personal organizers. Again the move prompted by an unfilled niche that Kate and Andy detected. Kate's may have been the first pink, neon-green, or coral-colored personal organizers on the market, an area that had been overwhelmingly drab—mostly dark brown, black or gray. The dressed-up organizers were given names: "Molly" (after Kate's sister), "Gabrielle," and "Elyce." "These are the first agendas I've seen that have a sense of style and wit to them," Andy said.

The stationery marketing began with a booklet-size catalog that introduced the address books, note cards, pencil cases, and erasers by telling the tale of "The Day Kate Missed a Tea." It was a tactic that, again, tied Kate's life, beauty, and style with the Kate Spade products. This kept the message very personal, associating the products with Kate, and not with a corporate mass-market image.

With the expansion—both geographical and into more cat-egories of products—Kate, Andy, Pamela, and Elyce needed to hire more help. "Figuring out what the four of us would do was easy," Kate said, since they were all friends. "We tended to think, 'Whatever needs to be done is the job.'" But when the business got bigger, "We needed to hire a second tier of managers, and that was harder." The new people needed to be assigned very specific responsibilities within the business, such as shipping or purchasing or retail. "When you hire peo-ple who've been at other companies," she explained, "they expect more formal direction and management."

They hired some people they knew and were comfortable with, such as Julia Leach, who worked with Andy when he was creative director at the advertising agency. By the end of 1997, Julia was handling planning for the retail outlets. By 2002, she was head of their creative services.

Early on, they established office rules that most people wouldn't associate with the high-pressure world of New York fashion. Using "please" and "thank you" was required, not just with clients, but with other employees. New hires were issued a copy of Emily Post's etiquette book, to urge people toward, in Post's words, "the continuous practice of kind impulses." Even though courtesy isn't really a habit limited to those from the Midwest, one of the three clocks in on the office wall was set to Kansas City time. (The other two were set to New York and Paris time.)

In mid-1999, Robin Marino was hired as president and chief operating officer (COO), a move that Kate later called "one of the smartest things we did." Marino, an experienced executive in the accessories business, had worked for Burberry Ltd., the luxury British fashion house, as well as for Donna Karan and Ralph Lauren. "Robin Marino is a great operator," Andy said at the time. "She'll be the point person, tying all the depart-ments together."

Before they found Marino, however, they experienced some rough patches. A year earlier, also with high expectations, they

Kate Spade poses with handbags and shoes
from her collection in New York, 2004.

had hired Stephen Ruzow as chief executive officer (CEO) after a long search. Up to then, Andy had been the chief executive. At fifty-four years old, Ruzow was much more experienced than Andy. He had been chief operating officer at Donna Karan, a $600 million company. When he was hired, Kate Spade was about a $25 million company.

But Ruzow left after three months. He and the four younger partners were not in accord about how to expand the company. He was later quoted in the *New York* as calling Kate and Andy "great kids," and saying they were "extremely conservative." Andy again assumed the double job of CEO and creative director.

While Ruzow was on board, the company brought its sales in-house to the headquarters on West Twenty-fifth Street, meaning the handbags were no longer sold through Cynthia O'Connor's showroom. O'Connor closed down her Manhattan showroom and became a consultant for the Spade company. She then was hired as an executive vice president of the company. However, she, too, left after just three months. She later filed a multimillion-dollar lawsuit, claiming she had been treated unfairly. A judge later ruled there was no fraud.

During this tumultuous time, after the missteps with Ruzow and O'Connor and before Robin Morino joined the company, the four partners took another big step. They sold 56 percent of their company to the luxury department store chain Neiman Marcus for $33.6 million. Kate, Andy, Elyce, and Pamela held on to the remaining 44 percent of the company and the right to control day-to-day operations. The move, in addition to making them financially secure, gave them the money to expand, both geographically and into other categories of fashion accessories. They were able to open more stores in the United States, and to look at expanding into Europe and more of Asia. They also wanted to begin designing shoes and eyeglasses. They even flirted with the idea of starting a clothing line, but after some experimenting, decided against it.

Kate designed some apparel, like pajamas and raincoats, but didn't try to go into clothing that requires more exact sizes.

In their personal life, Kate and Andy got a white Maltese terrier named Henry. The little dog joined them, *Vogue* magazine reported, on a night out at the Raccoon Lodge, a famously funky bar in their Tribeca neighborhood. Andy had enlisted a friend to get Kate a dog to celebrate their anniversary, and the yipping of a small, somewhat spoiled dog entered their lives. Kate later called Henry "the best anniversary gift I ever got." Kate indulged him so much that he showed up in numerous press reports over the years—looking like "a fashion accessory himself" and darting "from his master's lap to the red-painted toenails peeking from his mistress's lime-green mules."

A Kate Spade store in midtown Manhattan

6

Not ..
Advertising
is a Form of ..
Advertising

With the financial backing of Neiman Marcus, the Kate Spade company continued to grow. A big challenge was to stay personal and individual while becoming a multinational brand. "If we act like a big brand, consumers will reject us," Andy said at the time. The company was mostly relying on publicity from fashion magazines, and on Kate's in-store appearances. "Not advertising is a form of advertising," Andy explained. "It communicates to people 'I'm not corporate.'"

They continued to avoid most normal fashion advertising such as magazine ads. They got publicity with unusual projects, such as designing uniforms for the small airline, Song, an offshoot of Delta that lasted until 2006. In the 2002 television season, Kate played herself in an episode of Andy's brother's sit-com *Just Shoot Me!* A few years later, they publicized their collection with short narrative films projected on outdoor walls around Manhattan during Fashion Week. In one, a boy on a bicycle returns a woman's lost Kate Spade bag to her, after taking a blond wig from the bag and wearing it while he rides around the city. In another, two women, dressed identically and carrying Kate Spade gear, wander through a suburb until they meet up.

For the fall of 2002 line, Andy and Julia Leach designed a multipage magazine and film "narrative" about Tennessee Lawrence, a fictional twenty-something woman living in Manhattan. The story follows her during a weekend while her family visits from suburban Chicago. The Spades got some criticism for not showing enough of their products in the campaign, focusing instead on the narrative. "We're interested in promoting human connections with candor and confidence," Andy said. "Personal style plays a role in our campaigns, but always as a backdrop for honest, universally appreciated moments."

Kate and Andy's own story was well-enough known in the design world that it was no surprise that Tennessee's family was visiting from the Midwest, and that they were visiting their daughter in Manhattan. The connection to Kate was clear. "You know, when our parents would visit," she acknowledged at the time. "We would want to show them all the places we had discovered."

The tie between the Spades' work and their lives would cause some trouble a few years later, when a Kate Spade campaign featured a young woman quitting her job, leaving everything—including her boyfriend—behind, and moving to Switzerland. Rumors started immediately, and Andy had to do some damage control. "It has nothing to do with Kate," Andy told a reporter. "Her leaving me? No, no, no, no, absolutely not. It's not autobiographical."

More honors came Kate's way. Her bags were selected for an exhibit at the prestigious Cooper-Hewitt Design Museum in New York. A few years later, she was named one of *Glamour* magazine's 2002 "Women of the Year." Senator Hillary Rodham Clinton, the wife of former President Bill Clinton and later the secretary of state in the Obama administration, was on the same program as a presenter.

Chicago's Oak Street shopping district

Meanwhile, in what appeared to be a flurry of expansion, three new Kate Spade retail shops opened in late 2000. Actually, all of them had been in the works for months or even years, and they happened to be ready to open at once. In a two-week period, stores opened in Manhasset on Long Island in the Americana mall and in San Francisco in the Beaux Arts-style Shreve building. The Chicago store, which opened in November during the season's first snow flurries, was the largest yet, a 4,200-square-foot retail store in a historic townhouse in the upscale Oak Street shopping district. Counting a shop in Greenwich, Connecticut, which had opened in the summer, Kate Spade now had eight freestanding retail stores across the United States.

"It was really kind of luck that it all happened at the same time," Kate says, "and we'd hoped they would open (earlier). But we all know what construction is like." Andy added: "The truth is, we'd been looking in a lot of these cities for a couple of years. . . . But, it's always been a question of size and location. We want smaller spaces, and we want spaces with character.

In San Francisco, for example, we're in the Shreve Building, which is a historic landmark, but just off a high-traffic street." He adds, "We were just giddy when we found the space."

For the Chicago store, Kate and Andy hired Rogers and Marvel, along with interior designer Steven Sclaroff. Again, the store was designed to not look much like a retail shop— some of the interior walls were bright white and some were exposed red brick, with the wood floors stained dark. It gave the impression of a comfortable apartment. "We hired them," Andy says of the designers, "because they had no retail experience. The stores don't feel like stores; the fixtures don't look like fixtures."

Kate and Andy set the tone in the new stores with off-beat, one-of-a-kind items on display—things that you might find when you wander around a friend's home, picking up and looking at their favorite possessions—vintage books, flea-market discoveries, and unusual ceramic objects.

Both the Chicago and San Francisco stores devoted space to the Jack Spade collection, a men's line that Andy had been slowly developing. Andy had realized, in the same way Kate had, that the bag he'd really like to own was not in stores. "We started buying waxwear fabrics and heavy canvases to make a few bags for friends," he remembers. "Over time we received feedback on the function of the bags. . . . Then it occurred to us—why not sell bags to hardware stores and get feedback from people who really use utility bags?"

Jack Spade bags were sold through hardware stores starting in 1997. In December 1999, he had opened his first freestanding Jack Spade store, a five hundred-square-foot store on Greene Street in SoHo, designed by Sclaroff. Instead of press releases to announce the opening, Andy got noticed by sending out announcements in one hundred wallets stuffed with personal things that made them look used, like ticket stubs and photos. As in the Kate Spade stores, he placed quirky items around the store, but more masculine ones, such as an antique globe and a heavy lighter shaped like a dog. By the time the San Francisco and Chicago stores opened, the Jack Spade collection included big canvas messenger bags in several sizes, small sacks designed for camera gear, attaché cases, and computer bags.

Henry, Kate's little white Maltese, was described then by one reporter as the only member of the Spade household without his own designer line. But the report was not entirely accurate. In 2002, Kate designed matching rainwear for humans and dogs. The raincoat, rain-hat, and dog-coat were decorated with prints by Maira Kalman, the artist and author of children's books about the poet-dog, Max (*Ooh-la-la Max in Love, Max in Hollywood*, and *Max Makes a Million*). Kate and Maira's collaboration also produced canvas bags with illustrations by Kalman, who became a friend after she painted a portrait of Henry.

Meanwhile, Kate Spade eyeglasses and shoes were appearing in department stores, the result of licensing agreements. Kate also signed a licensing agreement for a line of Kate Spade beauty products with Estée Lauder, but it took more than two years for the products to get to market.

With shoes, Kate says, "It was just so surprisingly easy.'" She again used her "my-own-take-on-the-classics" method of design. She offered pointed-toe mules and a sandal trimmed with a single bead and incorporated fabrics already familiar to her—a pink herringbone, a sky-blue-and-pink silk pattern, as well as canvas, leather and ribbed faille.

In a parallel way, Kate designed eyeglass frames that she said were inspired by fashion icons like Greta Garbo and Jacqueline Kennedy Onassis. "Similar to bags, there can be a lot of personality in the eyewear category," Kate says. Her glasses took shapes like oversized squares, butterflies and aviators, and colors such as black, tortoise and olive. As with handbags, each style was given a name, emblazoned on the inside shaft of the temple piece.

Kate and Andy licensed other firms already in the business to manufacture her designs, rather than start from scratch as

Kate Spade green boots with a white bug detail

they had in handbags. "A new category is like going into a completely new business," Andy says, remembering the hard lessons he and Kate had learned. "Distribution is different. The product and process and manufacturing are different."

As to how they decided what new products to design, Kate said at the time: "We won't license the name or expand into a new area unless we think we can bring something new to a category that really makes it fresh. For instance, we got the idea to do raincoats after realizing that almost everything out there was in Burberry beige. So we decided to introduce a line of them using pink and turquoise."

After the deal with Neiman Marcus, Kate and Andy could afford to buy an apartment in Manhattan. They settled on a 3,000-square-foot, nine-room fixer-upper on Park Avenue at Seventy-seventh Street. The apartment had been part of an estate and had not been renovated in forty years. It still had much of its original woodwork.

Kate, Andy, and Henry the Maltese moved uptown. They had been living and working in lower Manhattan, in areas frequented by younger, hipper designers and artists. The Upper East Side is generally older, wealthier, and more staid. "In New York, people like to stereotype you by where you live," Kate says. "Our downtown friends kept saying. 'Oh, uptown, that's so provincial; it's not very modern.' It's so silly to be judged by your neighborhood. When I was growing up in Kansas City, you told people where you lived and they said, 'Oh, okay.' But in New York you tell them, and you hear this tone in their voices. It's ridiculous."

Steven Sclaroff, the designer for their stores, directed the renovation of their new home. True to the Spade creed, they respected the bones of the old apartment and tried to preserve its character while giving it a modern twist and modern comforts. They replaced the worn floors with the same refinished wood and redid the wiring, plumbing, kitchen and the baths. They decorated with nineteenth-century antique furniture as well as retro twentieth-century American pieces.

Kate Spade gold sandals

The Kansas City girl's wide-eyed-wonder at New York seemed to persist, even though at this point she was pretty much at the top of the design world. "Before I came to New York, I only had a few pictures of the city in my mind. And you know *That Girl?*" she says of the TV sit-com that ran during her girlhood. "Marlo Thomas jumping with her hat? I always loved that, and I wondered what that double street she crosses is. And it's Park Avenue! And that's what I can see out my window." But she kept her low-key midwesterner's perspective on the whole thing: "Not that we have some important view."

They had come a long way since Andy's homemade invitations warning their friends about the Heimlich maneuver. They were both approaching forty, so Kate threw a huge party for Andy two days before his birthday. She hired a chef, rented a loft space, commissioned a short film, and displayed photos of him as a kid. In one colorful touch, she ordered three hundred hand-embroidered cocktail napkins from Cabo San Lucas because she loved the bright hues she saw in Baja, Mexico, during their vacations.

In an unpleasant note during this time, Kate Spade's name was caught up twice in labor disputes at factories where her handbags were produced. In one, the workers, many of them poorly paid immigrants from the Dominican Republic and Ecuador, complained of six-day workweeks and eleven-hour workdays while making leather handbags for a subcontractor for the Kate Spade company. When they tried to unionize, which is their right under federal law, ten of the workers involved in the union-organizing were fired. The workers' pay and working conditions were the legal responsibility of the factory owner. But the workers said Kate must have known about the problems because the factory shared a building with her headquarters, and she regularly visited to check on the workmanship. Ultimately, the workers unionized, and the shop continued to produce Kate Spade bags. In the second labor controversy, workers who made Spade bags started organizing with a union. They said they had been working without overtime pay, health benefits, or holidays. The factory owner fired about fifty workers, mostly Latino immigrants, although some were rehired. The workers and their supporters picketed at the Kate Spade store in SoHo.

Kate was not the only designer caught up in labor troubles. Levi's, Nike, and many other upscale brands had been caught up in controversies about sweatshop conditions for workers in Mexico and Asia and even in the United States. It was bad publicity for the company. Critics focused on the contrast between the workers' low pay and working conditions and the high-priced handbags—as well as the $2.6 million Park Avenue apartment.

Kate Spade arrives at the 2002 Glamour Women of the Year Awards in New York.

7

I've **Never** seen anything Take Off So **Well**

To celebrate the tenth anniversary of their business, Kate and Andy threw a huge dinner party in the summer of 2003 at the Explorers Club headquarters, an old-fashioned building on the Upper East Side of Manhattan. The wood-paneled rooms feature memorabilia from the Explorers Club expeditions, such as a stuffed polar bear, a stuffed penguin, and a huge pair of tusks flanking a fireplace. The Spades documented the party for their fall advertising campaign, again connecting their life story with the story of their brand. The cake was shaped like the number ten, and they made up lists of their ten favorite places and ten favorite films.

For the employees, T-shirts were printed with, "They'll be out of business in a year." It was a reflection back, Andy says, on what people had said at the outset.

The Kate Spade brand was now a powerhouse in the design world. Sales hit $125 million in the 2003-2004 business year, including the handbag business and licensing income from shoes and eyewear. They were in the process of licensing beauty products and fragrances with Estée Lauder. Kate was designing a wide range of other products such as flatware and plates, bedding, and wallpaper and home textiles. Eventually, she developed a bridal collection that included coordinated bits from other categories—stationery for invitations, dinnerware and home décor for the registry, and shoes, clutches and other accessories for the wedding party.

About two hundred people worked for the company. The headquarters on West Twenty-fifth Street had gradually expanded to take up five floors of the building, with Kate's office one floor above Andy's. Less than ten years earlier, they had shipped bags from huge stacks in their tiny apartment.

Some of their hiring decisions were better than others. Andy remembers one particularly bad one, when he hired a warehouse supervisor without checking his references. "He turned out to be in the Cuban mafia and had shipped drugs out of the last job he had. And he was practicing voodoo on the employees. . . . We had to call federal people to come in while we told him to leave."

One of the Spades' goals was to expand internationally beyond their established business in Japan. So in early 2002, they hired a vice president in charge of international business development, Alan Goodman, who had been working for Ralph Lauren in a similar job. They also entered a partnership with a company called Globalluxe to handle business in Hong Kong, Korea, Taiwan, China, and Singapore. Another company, SSI, was signed up to handle business in the Philippines.

By the end of 2002, an 1,800-square-foot store had opened in a busy mall in Tsim Sha Tsui, one of Hong Kong's premiere shopping and tourist areas. The brightly lit shop was, once again, designed by the Rogers-Marvel architects. Some display cases were inspired by the modern painter Piet Mondrian, one of Kate's favorite artists. As in the stores in the United States, the décor included whimsical props like vintage magazines and books. Shortly after that, the first Kate Spade store in the Philippines opened in Manila's high-end Greenbelt

3 mall. The Spades were also interested in opening boutiques in Europe, starting with England, where Kate Spade products were selling well in high-end department stores such as Harvey Nichols.

Back at home in New York, Kate was selected in 2004 as one of *House Beautiful*'s "Giants of Design," a kind of funny designation for the five-foot-two Kate. The honor was in response to home products she had been rolling out over the past few years—first tableware, such as plates, flatware and glasses; then bedding, such as sheets and duvets; and finally household fabrics and wallpapers. Again, they had partnered with established companies.

"I have always loved accents, whether a bag, a vase, a journal, or a pillow," Kate says, describing the new designs as accessories for the home. "I have always found that personal style is best articulated through accessories."

It was no surprise, of course, that Kate and Andy became interested in designing articles for the home while remodeling and furnishing their Park Avenue apartment. "I hope it doesn't sound clichéd, but some of your best ideas come from trying to fill a void in your own life," Kate says. She had been frustrated with not finding what she wanted in wallpapers, home fabrics, even bedding and tableware. As usual, she looked for products that were timeless without being boring, a mix of traditional and modern. "In looking for dishes for our own apartment, we started thinking about dishes," Kate recalls. "Andy and I both worked on the collection, which kept it from being too masculine or too feminine."

In general, the designs were well received. A reviewer in Boston described the tableware as "mildly eccentric dishes Alice in Wonderland would have liked for her tea party." A set of cups had a pattern around the rim that mimicked the contrasting-color stitching found on some of Kate's handbags. A wineglass was etched with unevenly spaced rings on the stem. Dragonflies decorated some plates. And one china set

Early morning on the Tsim Sha Tsui Promenade in Kowloon, Hong Kong, China

used Kate's familiar rich, bright colors—aqua, yellow, and coral—as spot decorations.

Consumers responded as well. "Kate Spade flatware is doing extremely well," one buyer for a big department store chain said. "In my 25-year career, I've never seen anything take off so well."

In the years immediately following the September 11, 2001, terrorist attacks, many Americans cut back on traveling and focused instead on making their homes more comforting, their kitchens more welcoming. Tableware from the designer Vera Wang arrived in stores at about the same time as Kate's. The two collections are credited with spicing up tableware departments, which had traditionally been pretty staid.

As if she didn't have enough on her plates, Kate signed with the publisher Simon & Schuster to write three books on style and etiquette. The books—*Style*, *Manners*, and *Occasions*—were petite, easy to read, with little line-drawing illustrations. Just about the right size to slip into a purse, the books convey Kate's down-to-earth and fun-loving philosophy with very specific advice.

Manners expresses the creed that courtesy is nothing more than trying to be kind to others and put them at ease. "Showing respect is a gift, one that costs nothing and is endlessly appreciated." "In mixed company, some words are best left unsaid, such as short, bald, fat, skinny, still single, and unemployed."

Occasions takes up where *Manners* leaves off, with making people welcome in your home. "Once your guests arrive, get thee out of the kitchen! . . . They have come to be with you, not your veal scaloppini, no matter how good it tastes."

Style covers how to make it all look good—when you're at home, at work, or at play. "As the most restful color in the spectrum, green evokes the safety of traffic lights, the calm of nature, and Kermit's easy grin."

Kate used her standard technique of starting the books with something classic—advice from Emily Post and William

Kate's books focus on etiquette and manners.

Strunk, co-author of *The Elements of Style*, a famous book about writing well. She then added a dash of more modern concerns—how to politely use cell phones, call waiting, and e-mail. The books contained advice you can use, or you wish others would use, much of it simple courtesy, such as park your shopping cart next to the shelf, not in the middle of the aisle, in the grocery store. But some of it is really just for fun, like providing the French translation—for the polite traveler abroad—of "I'd like to check my raincoat and my small dog, Edna."

The three new books were their first venture with a major publisher. Earlier, they had published a limited number of books for their stores. *Contents*, a photo book from 2000, documented forty-six women—some famous and some not—by looking at the contents of their purses. Some were highly organized, some really messy. It was a unique way of drawing women's portraits. "It occurred to us that the items in your handbag essentially define who you are and what is important to you," Kate says. "We wondered, 'Would women from

all walks of life be willing to show us their personal possessions, their keepsakes, their car keys?'"

In a similar vein, Andy had produced *Honesty*, a book that
documented what happened to one hundred wallets dropped
on the streets of Manhattan. As he explains it: "We filled the
wallets up in a real way and dropped 25 off on the Upper
East Side, 25 on the Upper West Side, 25 on the Lower East
Side, 25 on the Lower West Side. And we photographed as
people found them to see who returned them, to see whether
the Upper East Side is more honest than the Lower East Side.
. . . at the same time, we put up fliers that said, 'Lost Jack
Spade wallet,' so that was kind of an outdoor ad." He sold the
Honesty book alongside his Jack Spade line.

In 2003, Kate won the FiFi Award for Bath & Body Line
of the Year. The FiFis are the "Oscars of the fragrance world,"
and Kate won for her new collection of perfumes, bath products, and moisturizers. The beauty collection took more than
two years to get to market after she signed the licensing agreement in 1999 with Estée Lauder. She had been involved in
every aspect of production, from developing the fragrances
to designing bottles and packages.

She wanted to formulate "a simple, feminine, timeless perfume." The main fragrance was white honeysuckle. "I still
remember smelling it on long car trips with my family," she
reminisces. In addition, the scent included touches of garde-
nia, jasmine, tuberose, and a half-dozen other perfume "notes."
Kate wanted to make sure everything was exactly to her taste.
"With some designers, you do a few options and let them pick,"
the partner at Estée Lauder said at the time. "With Kate, she
was in there picking notes and meeting with us once and twice
a week to get it all right."

Kate even designed the inside of the boxes the perfume
bottles came in. "It's like Kate's bags—the linings are always
unexpected and special," Andy said. They added little sayings
on the boxes, such as, "she likes a long bath and a short story.
On some of the tags, we have things like, 'Call your mother,'

which seems to amuse our customers. We thought it would be fun to try that on the fragrance packaging."

Kate launched the beauty line with a six-week, ten-city tour of in-store appearances around the United States and Europe. The last stop took her to England and Harrods, the London department store. On the tour, Kate was treated like a fashion star. She signed fragrance bottles, wallets, handbags, and even Kate Spade shoes, for customers. At one stop, a particularly avid fan reportedly passed up her own wedding rehearsal luncheon in order to meet Kate.

A model wears Kate Spade ruby patent leather high-heeled Mary Janes.

8

I'm Not Worrying as Much

Kate mentioned to a reporter as early as 1999 that she'd like to have children, but it wasn't until February 2005 that Frances Beatrix Spade was born. Kate was forty-two.

"It was something we always wanted to do, but you get caught up in the moment of the business," Kate said just before baby Bea's birth. "This industry is very, very competitive," Andy added, "and I didn't want to feel guilty about not spending time with a child. But now, we have a business, and it's strong. So I think there's an advantage to being our age and at this point in our lives. We can do this."

After Bea was born Kate started relaxing a bit about work. "There's a bigger responsibility in place and, honestly, I'm not worrying as much," she said, while talking about her fall 2005 offerings. Called "Collect," the fall line was something of a change for her, more high-end and with upscale materials—such as python and brightly colored snakeskin. They were far removed from the suburban American retro feel that defined much of her earlier work. The new collection also broke new ground in pricing. "We were very conscious in the past of keeping the signature collection accessibly priced," she said at the time. "But with Collect, I'm allowing myself to be free and kind of unconcerned about those things. Now I'm thinking, Let's have fun." She used spotted calfskin, shells, crystals. "It's throwing caution to the wind, and not being restricted by price." The new collection wasn't a total change. It was similar to her previous work in keeping a sense of humor and using unexpected accents.

She was relaxed enough—both at work and at home—that six months after baby Bea's birth, she hadn't fixed up the baby's nursery. "By the time I get around to it," she laughed, "Bea will be wanting posters of a boy band."

It was no surprise when Kate began designing a line of baby clothes to go along with the earlier strollers and diaper bags.

Other changes for the company were on the horizon as well. Neiman Marcus, which at that time was considered the top American chain of luxury department stores, had owned a majority share of Kate Spade for six years, allowing Kate and Andy to do their work and expand pretty much at their own pace. In spring 2005, just a few months after Bea's birth, Neiman Marcus was bought by two investment firms for about $5.1 billion. It was a time of huge mergers, acquisitions, and leveraged buyouts in the business world. Companies could borrow money easily, and buy other companies. But then, instead of being able to carry on at a slow, methodical pace, the new owners were burdened by huge debt payments. They were under pressure to expand and make more money quickly. They could also sell parts of the company to raise cash.

Within a few months, the new owners of Neiman Marcus began trying to sell Kate Spade. It was an unsettled time. Neiman Marcus and the Kate Spade company put out a joint press release expressing optimism about the future but saying, "There could be no assurance that this process will result in any specific transaction." The Kate Spade company was on the market for a year—a long time in the current business environment.

Neiman Marcus once owned the majority of Kate Spade but was bought by investment firms in 2005 and began to look to sell the company to raise capital.

Meanwhile, their flagship shop on Broome Street in SoHo was remodeled into much larger 2,600-square-foot store. The company also announced plans to open as many as fifty stores in the next five years. For a retail operation at the time, that wasn't overly ambitious—the chain Coach had plans for 280 retail stores—but it was a lot faster than they had been expanding. In the first twelve years, Kate and Andy had opened only twenty stores. The company also announced plans to go into ready-to-wear clothing. They also relaunched the stationery category, this time with the licensing partner Crane & Co., and got into other categories, such as Kate Spade pet dishes.

Reports surfaced over the next year of various unsuccessful negotiations to sell the company. Some reports speculated the selling price was too high, or that the sale was complicated by the fact that Kate, Andy, Pamela, and Elyce owned 44 percent of the company. Then, in fall 2006, the four Kate Spade partners sold their share of the company to Neiman Marcus for a reported $59 million. Now Neiman Marcus owned the company outright and were then able to sell the entire company to Liz Claiborne Inc. for about $124 million.

Kate, Andy, Pamela, and Elyce remained with the company after Claiborne bought it. Kate and Andy signed a "service agreement" to stay in their roles as designer and CEO until mid-2007, helping to make a smooth transition. Claiborne, a $5 billion company, already owned other brands, such as Juicy Couture, Mexx, and Lucky Brand Jeans. Claiborne announced ambitious plans to open two hundred Kate Spade stores in North American, Europe, and Asia.

Some commentators said Kate Spade had lost its way by pricing its products too high for its target customers, the so-called "bridge" market below high-end designers but above department store retail. Others said they had strayed too far from handbags and that Andy was focused too much on his off-beat projects and not enough on the company's core products.

But, as one writer pointed out, "What outsiders don't quite understand is that on some level, Kate and Andy don't really give a damn. It's not that they don't want to build a bigger, more successful company—they do. But empire-building in conventional terms? Sorry, not their cup of tea. More than anything, Kate and Andy want to stay true to what they built— even if it means settling for a smaller piece of the pie."

Soon it no longer mattered to Kate and Andy what their critics said. Nine months after the Liz Claiborne purchase, when they had fulfilled their service agreement, they left the company.

Later they described how they had decided to leave the business. They did an experiment and counted the number of decisions they had to make in one day. It turned out to be 266, from "How many rhinestones?" to "Whom should we hire?" to "What shade of pink?" Andy's response after the experiment was "Ugh." They looked at baby Bea, looked at what was fun in their lives and what wasn't, and decided, along with Pamela and Elyce, to slow down their lives.

After the sale, the four former partners, along with their families, took a well-earned vacation to Cabo San Lucas in Baja, Mexico. "We were there for a week," Elyce remembers, "and we didn't once talk about the sale."

After the sale Kate and Andy could focus on whatever interested them. For Andy, wide-ranging projects pulled him in several directions—producing films, working with bikes, making wine, experimenting with his new shop in SoHo called Partners & Spade, as well as publishing books of photos from his iPhone.

For Kate, life mostly revolved around activities with Beatrix such as skating, music classes, and play-dates with other children.

Kate's design sense was still very much intact, if focused slightly more domestically—she made a point of cutting her daughter's sandwiches into heart shapes.

"The other mothers are like, 'Okay, whatever,' They think I'm insane," she says. "But I want to be able to do this while I can. When she's like, 'Mom, get away from me!' then I'll think about what else I want to do, but I'm incredibly glad I can do this now."

Does she miss the high-pressure design world? "I haven't even been into a Kate Spade shop since we left."

And what's the response from her friends in the business? Suzanne Martine, the woman who gave Kate her first job at *Mademoiselle,* puts it this way: "You made it out! Alive!"

Timeline

1962:	Born on December 24 in Kansas City, Missouri.
1985:	Graduates with a degree in journalism from Arizona State University.
1986-1992:	Works at *Mademoiselle* magazine.
1993:	Starts Kate Spade company with Andy Spade; shows six handbags at accessories show; gets first orders from Barneys and Charivari.
1995:	Marries Andy Spade.
1996:	Wins Top New Talent Award from Council of Fashion Designers of America; opens first freestanding Kate Spade retail store in SoHo.
1998:	Wins Accessory Designer of the Year award from Council of Fashion Designers of America.
1999:	Sells a majority share of Kate Spade company to Neiman Marcus; begins designing shoes, eyewear, tableware, bedding, and beauty products.
2004:	Publishes books on etiquette and style.
2005:	Daughter, Frances Beatrix Spade, is born.
2006:	Sells remaining stake in Kate Spade company to Neiman Marcus.
2007:	Leaves Kate Spade company.

Sources

Chapter One | You Never Grow Out of a Purse

p. 11-12, "a tedious landscape . . ." Linda Tishchler, "Power Couple," *Fast Company*, March 1, 2005.

p. 11, "figuring out a way . . ." Kate Spade, *Style* (New York: Simon & Schuster, 2004), 10.

p. 11 "My mother thought . . ." Ellyn Spragins, "Kate and Andy Spade: How We Bagged Our Careers," *Fortune Small Business*, September 1, 2003.

p. 12, "Even when I was . . ." Spade, *Style*, 52.

p. 12, "When I was a . . ." Susan C. Ryan, "For Designer Kate Spade, Success Is in the Bag," *Boston Globe*, July 14, 1999.

p. 12, "My mother used . . ." Heather Bracher Severs, "A Designer's Mother's Day," *Town & Country*, May 2000.

p. 12, "You never grow . . ." Alex Witchel, "New Kit Bags, to Send Troubles Packing," *New York Times*, December 16, 2001.

p. 12, "She had clutches . . ." Rebecca Brown Burton, "Kate Spade," *Time*, February 16, 2004.

p. 14, "They brought their . . ." Spragins, "Kate and Andy Spade: How We Bagged Our Careers."

p. 14, "leadership, self-confidence . . ." Web site of St. Teresa's Academy.

p. 14, "I wanted to . . ." Elisabeth Bumiller, "A Cautious Rise to a Top Name in Fashion," *New York Times*, March 12, 1999.

p. 14, "I loved fashion . . ." Ibid.

p. 15, "'You can't wear . . ." Honor Brodie, "Spade in the Shade," *InStyle*, August 1, 2002.

p. 15, "I was a . . ." Spragins, "Kate and Andy Spade: How We Bagged Our Careers."

p. 16, "It was love . . ." Michelle Granger and Tina Sterling, *Fashion Entrepreneurship* (New York: Fairchild Publications, 2003), 320.

p. 16, "In 1986 . . ." Spragins, "Kate and Andy Spade: How We Bagged Our Careers."

p. 16, "Andy stayed in . . ." Ibid.

p. 16, "Yo quiero . . ." Emily Dougherty, "Lady Spade," *Harper's Bazaar*, April 2000.

p. 17, "I love, love, love . . ." Julia Reed, "Miss Congeniality," *Vogue*, August 2004.

p. 17, "Kate had just . . ." Spragins, "Kate and Andy Spade: How We Bagged Our Careers."

Chapter Two | How Hard Can It Be?

p. 21, "We've seen the people . . ." Ron Lieber, *Upstart Start-ups: How 34 Young Entrepreneurs Overcame Youth, Inexperience, and Lack of Money to Create Thriving Businesses* (New York: Broadway Books, 1998), 8.

p. 21, "It was less . . ." Bart Boehlert, "Kate Spade and Her Hip Handbags," *Urban Desires*, April-May 1996.

p. 22,   "He asked . . ." Jackie White, "For Kate Spade, Success Is in the Bag," *Buffalo News*, December 28, 1997.

p. 22,   "It was rectangular . . ." Ryan, "For Designer Kate Spade, Success Is in the Bag."

p. 22,   " There was a lot . . ." Lieber, *Upstart Start-ups*, 24-25.

p. 23,   "I didn't have . . ." Ibid, 143-144.

p. 25,   "To have borrowed . . ." "In the Groove With Kate Spade," *Fortune Small Business*, February 1, 2000.

p. 25,   "When I left . . ." Boehlert, "Kate Spade and Her Hip Handbags."

p. 25,   "Our friends were . . ." Spragins, "Kate and Andy Spade: How We Bagged Our Careers."

p. 25,   "I sat down . . ." Spragins, "Kate and Andy Spade: How We Bagged Our Careers."

p. 25,   "I neurosed over . . ." Bumiller, "A Cautious Rise to a Top Name in Fashion."

p. 26,   "Handbags should be . . ." Ryan, "For Designer Kate Spade, Success Is in the Bag."

p. 26,   "Picture a square . . ." Ibid.

p. 26,   "Since I had seen . . ." Bumiller, "A Cautious Rise to a Top Name in Fashion."

p. 26,   "I tried a lot . . ." Lieber, *Upstart Start-ups*, 43-44.

p. 26-27,   "They make a . . ." Spragins, "Kate and Andy Spade: How We Bagged Our Careers."Ellyn. Ibid.

p. 30,   "Once I started . . ." Lieber, *Upstart Start-ups*, 144.

p. 30,   "One (fabric supplier) . . ." Burton, "Kate Spade."

p. 30,   "I loved Olive . . ." Ryan, "For Designer Kate Spade, Success Is in the Bag."

p. 30,   "Andy kept saying . . ." Ibid.

p. 30,   "He'll never . . ." Amy Larocca, "The Spades' New Bag." *New York* magazine, February 14, 2010.

Chapter Three | It Didn't Cover the Cost of the Show

p. 34,   "The people with . . ." Lieber, *Upstart Start-ups,* 63.

p. 34,   "We moved in . . ." Spragins, "Kate and Andy Spade: How We Bagged Our Careers."

p. 34,   "There was something . . . " Ryan, "For Designer Kate Spade, Success Is in the Bag."

p. 34,   "You can imagine . . ." Ibid.

p. 34,   "But it didn't . . ." Bumiller, "A Cautious Rise to a Top Name in Fashion."

p. 36,   "We were on . . ." Ryan, "For Designer Kate Spade, Success Is in the Bag."

p. 36,   "The great thing . . ." Lieber, *Upstart Start-ups*, 63.

p. 36,   "Spade, whose philsophy . . ." Ryan, "For Designer Kate Spade, Success Is in the Bag."

p. 38,   "They sold quickly . . ." Spragins, "Kate and Andy Spade: How We Bagged Our Careers."

p. 38,   "I remember Barneys . . ." Ibid.
p. 38,   "We wanted to . . ." Ibid.
p. 39,   "Most people wont . . ." Lieber, *Upstart Start-ups*, 144.
p. 39,   "When you show . . ." Spragins, "Kate and Andy Spade: How We Bagged Our Careers."
p. 39,   "Kate Spade's trendy . . ." C. R. Constance White, "Patterns," *New York Times*, June 6, 1995.
p. 39,   "Designers used to . . ." Ibid.
p. 42,   "was a decision . . ." Spragins, "Kate and Andy Spade: How We Bagged Our Careers."
p. 42,   "It was going . . ." Ibid.
p. 42,   "was all for it . . ." Spade, *Occasions*, 10.
p. 42   "sealed with a sticker . . ." Kate Spade, *Occasions* (New York: Simon & Schuster, 2004), 47.
p. 43,   "The question is . . ." Lieber, *Upstart Start-ups*, 110.
p. 43,   "The flowers were great . . ." Spade, *Occasions*, 107.
p. 43,   "Whatever notions . . ." Ibid., 11

Chapter Four | Huge Growth We Didn't Expect

p. 45,   "As if Audrey Hepburn . . ." Witchel, "New Kit Bags, to Send Troubles Packing."
p. 45-46, "I look back . . ." Larocca, "The Spades' New Bag."
p. 46,   "The evening's most . . ." Boehlert, "Kate Spade and Her Hip Handbags."
p. 47,   "If you can't . . ." "Bags on the Brain: purse lady Kate Spade is mad about hue," *People*, June 3, 1996.
p. 47-48, "Kate Spade says . . ." Wendy Hessen, "Rites of spring," *Women's Wear Daily*, October 21, 1996.
p. 48,   "Now Andy gets . . ." Tischler, "Power Couple."
p. 49,   "those Indian bead . . ." Wendy Hessen, "Kate Spade digs SoHo," *Women's Wear Daily*, July 8, 1996.
p. 49,   "besides cementing our . . ." Ibid.
p. 49,   "Andy Spade Becomes . . ." "Andy Spade," *Adweek* (Eastern Edition), October 7, 1996.
p. 49,   "Spade Times Two . . ." "Spade Times Two," *Women's Wear Daily*, September 16, 1996.
p. 51,   "I decided to . . ." Spragins, "Kate and Andy Spade: How We Bagged Our Careers."
p. 51-52, "It's instinct . . ." Maryann Lorusso, "Playing her Cards," *Footwear News*, July 19, 1999.
p. 52,   "Back in the . . ." "In the Groove With Kate Spade," *Fortune Small Business*, February 1, 2000.
p. 53,   "Such a status . . ." Wendy Goodman, "Style in Spades," *New York* magazine *Online*, June 11, 2001.
p. 55,   "People have to . . ." Vivian Chen, "Fake is out of Fashion," *Corporate Counsel*, May 2003.
p. 58,   "We were running . . ." Spragins, "Kate and Andy Spade: How We Bagged Our Careers."

p. 58,   "We had to . . ." Ibid.
p. 58,   "It was difficult . . ." Brodie, "Spade in the Shade."
p. 58,   "We fell in love . . ." Goodman, "Style in Spades."

Chapter Five | Whatever Needs to Be Done is the Job

p. 62,   "There wasn't one . . ." Wendy Hessen, "The Spade Ascent," *Women's Wear Daily*, October 20, 1997.
p. 63,   "We call our . . ." Ibid.
p. 64,   "We can't really . . ." David Moin, "Kate Spade Set to Open 2 New Stores," *Women's Wear Daily*, January 28, 2000.
p. 64,   "These are the . . ." Dina Santorelli, "Kate Spade digs new line," *HFN The Weekly Newspaper for the Home Furnishing Network*, March 2, 1998.
p. 65,   "Figuring out what . . ." Spragins, "Kate and Andy Spade: How We Bagged Our Careers."
p. 65,   "one of the . . ." Ibid.
p. 65,   "Robin Marino is . . ." David Moin, "Robin Marino Joining Spade as President," *Women's Wear Daily*, April 12, 1999.
p. 68,   "great kids," Bumiller, "A Cautious Rise to a Top Name in Fashion."
p. 69,   "the best anniversary . . ." Spade, *Occasions*, 92 .
p. 69,   "a fashion accessory . . ." Leslie Kaufman, "In my .... Satchel: Kate Spade," *New York Times*, June   20, 1999.
p. 69,   "from his master's . . ." Brodie, "Spade in the Shade."

Chapter Six | Not Advertising is a Form of Advertising

p. 71,   "If we act . . ." David Moin, "Neiman Marcus Group Negotiating to Acquire Kate Spade Handbags," *Women's Wear Daily*, January 22, 1999.
p. 72,   "We're interested in . . ." Lisa Sanders, "New approach for Kate Spade; Narrative used to sell accessories," *Advertising Age*, August 5, 2002.
p. 72,   "You know, when . . ." Jackie White, "Kate Spade: The Woman and the Brand Share a Flexible Nature," *Kansas City Star*, September 10, 2002.
p. 72,   "It has nothing . . ." Marc Karimzadeh, "Kate Spade Sets a New Course," *Women's Wear Daily*,   August 16, 2004.
p. 73-74, "It was really . . ." Janet Ozzard, "Kate Spade's Retail Roadshow," *Women's Wear Daily*, November 6, 2000.
p. 74,   "We were just . . ." Diane Dorrans Saeks, "Spade Suits San Francisco: New Accessories Store Caters to Men with Jack Spade Line and a   'Husband Chair,'" *Daily News Record,* December 11, 2000.
p. 74,   "We hired them . . ." Lisa Bertagnoli, "Kate Spade Opens in Chicago," *Women's Wear Daily*, November 22, 2000.
p. 74,   "We started buying . . ." Official Web site of Jack Spade, http://www.jackspade.com.

p. 75,   "It was just so . . ." Jackie White, "Kate Spade Goes Beyond Hand Bags," *Kansas City Star*, April 20, 2000.

p. 75,   "Similar to bags . . ." Melanie Kletter, "Kate Spade Inks Deal for Eyewear License," *Women's Wear Daily*, March 28, 2000.

p. 78,   "A new category . . ." Spragins, "Kate and Andy Spade: How We Bagged Our Careers."

p. 78,   "We won't license . . ." "In the Groove With Kate Spade," *Fortune Small Business*.

p. 78,   "In New York . . ." Annette Tapert, "Kate's Place: Designer Kate Spade Brings a Dash of her   Trademark Whimsy to a Park Avenue Classic," *Town & Country*, October 2004.

p. 80,   "Before I came . . ." Larocca, "The Spades' New Bag."

Chapter Seven | I've Never Seen Anything Take Off So Well

p. 83,   "They'll be out . . ." A. Scott Walton, "Style: A Clothing Line Not in Cards for Kate Spade's Empire," *Atlanta Journal-Constitution*, October 26, 2003.

p. 84,   "He turned out . . ." Mae Anderson, "On the Spot Andy Spade," *Adweek* (Eastern Edition), November 18, 2002.

p. 85,   "I have always . . ." "Kate Spade Announces the Launch of kate spade Home; Company Signs Licensing Agreements with Scalamandre, Lenox, And Springs," *Business Wire*, June 9, 2003.

p. 85,   "I hope it . . ." Roslyn Sulcas, "Giants of design," *House Beautiful*, June 2004.

p. 85,   "In looking for . . ." Kristen Paulson, "Kate Spade Comes Home," *Boston Globe*, February 5, 2004.

p. 85,   "mildly eccentric . . ." Paulson, "Kate Spade Comes Home."

p. 88,   "Kate Spade flatware . . ." Carla Webb and Allison Zisko, "Flatware lines From Vera Wang and Kate Spade Benefit From the Collections' Popularity and Cross-Merchandising Opportunities," *HFN The Weekly Newspaper for the Home Furnishing Network*, September 5, 2005.

p. 88,   "Showing respect is . . ." Kate Spade, *Manners* (New York: Simon & Schuster, 2004), 14, 48.

p. 88,   "Once your guests . . ." Spade, *Occasions*, 58.

p. 88,   "As the most . . ." Spade, *Style*, 32.

p. 89,   "I'd like to . . ." Spade, *Manners*, 95.

p. 89-90, "It occurred to us . . ." Lauren David Peden, "The Inner Lives of Purses," *New York Times*, November 19, 2000.

p. 90,   "We filled the wallets . . ." Anderson, "On the Spot Andy Spade."

p. 90,   "I still remember . . ." Julie Naughton, "Kate's New Bag," *Women's Wear Daily*, February 8, 2002.

p. 90,   "With Kate . . ." Ibid.

p. 90-91, "It's like Kate's . . ." Ibid.

Chapter Eight | I'm Not Worrying as Much

p. 93,   "It was something . . ." Tishchler, "Power Couple."

p. 93,   "There's a bigger . . ." Venessa Lau, "Collect Call: Kate Spade is sitting pretty with a luxurious new line and baby to boot(ie)," *W*, September 2005.

p. 93-94, "We were very . . ." Ibid.

p. 94,   "By the time . . ." Ibid.

p. 94,   "There could be no . . ." Sophia Chabbott, "Kate Spade on the Block: NMG Eyes Strategic Options," *Women's Wear Daily*, September 19, 2005.

p. 96,   "What outsiders don't . . ." Tishchler, "Power Couple."

p. 96,   "Ugh," Larocca, "The Spades' New Bag."

p. 97,   "We were there . . ." Ibid.

p. 97,   "The other mothers . . ." Ibid.

p. 97,   "I haven't even . . ." Ibid.

p. 97,   "You made it . . ." Ibid.

Bibliography

Abbey, Cherie, ed. "Kate Spade." Biography *Today* 16, no. 2 (April 2007).

Anderson, Mae. "On the Spot Andy Spade." *Adweek*, November 18, 2002.

"Andy Spade becomes president of Kate Spade Handbags." *Adweek*, October 7, 1996.

"Bags on the Brain: Purse lady Kate Spade is mad about hue." *People Weekly*, June 3, 1996.

Baker, John F. "Etiquette la Spade." *Publishers Weekly*, November 18, 2002.

Bertagnoli, Lisa. "Kate Spade Opens in Chicago." *Women's Wear Daily*, November 22, 2000.

Boehlert, Bart. "Kate Spade and Her Hip Handbags." *Urban Desires*, April-May 1996. http://desires.com/2.1/Style/Spade/Docs/spade1.html.

Brodie, Honor. "Spade in the Shade." *InStyle*, August 1, 2002.

Bumiller, Elisabeth. "A Cautious Rise to a Top Name in Fashion." *New York Times*, March 12, 1999.

Burton, Rebecca Brown. "Kate Spade." *Time*, February 16, 2004.

Business Wire. "Kate Spade Announces Asian Expansion; Company Signs Distribution Rights Agreements With Globalluxe and Store Specialists, Inc." *Business Wire*, Oct. 14, 2002.

———. "Kate Spade Announces the Launch of kate spade Home; Company Signs Licensing Agreements with Scalamandre, Lenox, And Springs." *Business Wire*, June 9, 2003.

———. "The Neiman Marcus Group Acquires Interest in Manufacturer of Kate Spade Handbags." *Business Wire*, February 4, 1999.

"Candid Camera." *W*, September 2000.

Chabbott, Sophia. "An Accessories Boost: Liz Claiborne Acquiring Kate Spade for $125M." *Women's Wear Daily*, November 8, 2006.

———. "Kate Spade Negotiations: Slow and Steady." *Women's Wear Daily*, July 11, 2006.

———. Chabbott, Sophia. "Mother of Invention: Kate Spade Eyes Growth Amid Sale Buzz." *Women's Wear Daily*, July 25, 2005.

———. Chabbott, Sophia. "Kate Spade on the Block: NMG Eyes Strategic Options." *Women's Wear Daily*, September 19, 2005.

"CFDA Board Taps Wang, Von Furstenberg, Spade." *Women's Wear Daily*, July 1,1999.

Chen, Vivia. "Fake is out of Fashion." *Corporate Counsel*, May 2003.

Cohen, Edie. "SoHo simple: Rogers Marvel creates an expanded shop for Kate Spade." *Interior Design*, April 1998.

———. "Ace of Spades." *Interior Design*. April 2001.

Cosmetics International. "Estee Lauder Bags a New Perfect Partner." *Cosmetics International*, November 25, 1999.

Dougherty, Emily. "Lady Spade." *Harper's Bazaar*, April 2000.

Dunaief, Daniel. "Counterfeit Retail Knockoffs Cost New York Billions in Lost Revenue." *Daily News*, November 23, 2004.

Edelson, Sharon. "SoHo Getting Designer Look." *Women's Wear Daily*, April 1, 1997.

Embry, Liz. "Style: Fashion Designers Set Their Talents on the Home Dining Table." *Houston Chronicle*, March 24, 2004.

"Fashion Scoops." *Women's Wear Daily*, March 10, 2004.

———. *Women's Wear Daily*, April 9, 2004.

———. *Women's Wear Daily*, May 17, 2004.

Geran, Monica. "It's in the Bag." *Interior Design*, April 1997.

Granger, Michelle, and Tina Sterling. *Fashion Entrepreneurship*. New York: Fairchild Publications, 2003.

Goodman, Wendy. "Style in Spades." *New York* magazine *Online*, June 11, 2001. http://www.newyorkmetro.com/nymetro/urban/home/design/features/4793.

Hanson, Holly. "Awards Going to Younger Designers." *Houston Chronicle*, January 15, 1998.

Hayt, Elizabeth. "The Designer." *New York Times*, July 30, 2000.

Hessen, Wendy. "Eyeing Kate Spade." *Women's Wear Daily*, November 13, 2000.

———. "Kate Spade Digs SoHo." *Women's Wear Daily*, July 8, 1996.

———. "Ruzow Joins Kate Spade in CEO Post." *Women's Wear Daily*, March 16, 1998.

———. "Ruzow Quits Spade After 3-Month Stint." *Women's Wear Daily*, July 6, 1998.

———. "Sales Rep Files $8.5 Million Suit on Kate Spade." *Women's Wear Daily*, January 28, 1999.

———. "The Spade Ascent: Handbag company Kate Spade plots its growth with new products, retail and licensing deals." *Women's Wear Daily*, October 20, 1997.

"In the Bag." *Women's Wear Daily*, June 5, 2003.

"In Brief: Marino Out at Kate Spade." *Women's Wear Daily*, May 12, 2005.

"In the Groove With Kate Spade: The chic handbag maker and husband Andy are hot with the fashionistas. But can they grow and remain the rage at the same time?" *Fortune Small Business*, February 1, 2000.

Iovine, Julie V. "Kate Spades That Are Best Left at Home, Not Slung Over the Shoulder." *New York Times*, November 13, 2003.

Karimzadeh, Marc. "Kate Spade Sets a New Course." *Women's Wear Daily*, August 16, 2004

"Kate Spade Plans 15 Units in Asian Expansion." *Women's Wear Daily*, December 9, 2002.

Kaufman, Leslie. "In my …. Satchel: Kate Spade." *New York Times*, June 20, 1999.

Kerwin, Jessica. "Aces of Spade: Producing films, books and even conceptual art, Kate and Andy Spade push their brand to its limit." *W*, August, 2003.

Kletter, Melanie. "Kate Spade Inks Deal for Eyewear License." *Women's Wear Daily*, March 28, 2000.

———. "Kate Spade's New Path." *Women's Wear Daily*, November 19, 2001.

———. "New Horizons for Kate Spade." *Women's Wear Daily*, November 25, 2002.

"Labels for less." *Financial Times,* August 23, 1999.

Lach, Jennifer. "Let's Get Personal." *American Demographics*, February 1999.

Laing, Jennifer. "Hello Mother, Hello Fido." *New York Times*, October 27, 2002.

Larocca, Amy. "The Spades' New Bag." *New York* magazine, February 14, 2010.

Lau, Venessa. "Collect Call: Kate Spade is sitting pretty with a luxurious new line and baby to boot(ie)." *W,* September 2005.

Lazaro, Marvin. "Kate Spade Fashions Home Line." *Home Textiles Today*, November 5, 2001.

"What It Costs to Make a Handbag." *New York Times* (Letter to the Editor), September. 25, 1999.

Lieber, Ron. *Upstart Start-Ups: How 34 Young Entrepreneurs Overcame Youth, Inexperience, and Lack of Money to Create Thriving Businesses.* New York: Broadway Books, 1998.

Lockwood, Lisa. "Winners' Circle." *Women's Wear Daily,* November 1, 2002.

Lorusso, Maryann. "Playing Her Cards." *Footwear News,* July 19, 1999.

Moin, David. "Kate Spade Set to Open 2 New Stores." *Women's Wear Daily*, January 28, 2000.

————. "Neiman Marcus Group Negotiating to Acquire Kate Spade Handbags." *Women's Wear Daily*, January 22, 1999.

————. "NM Acquires 56% of Kate Spade." *Women's Wear Daily,* February 5, 1999.

————. "Robin Marino Joining Spade as President." *Women's Wear Daily*, April 12, 1999.

————. "The Neiman's Challenge: Staying at Top of Luxury Under Two New Owners." *Women's Wear Daily*, May 3, 2005.

Mooney, Jennifer. "Blasting Off; Handbag Maven Kate Spade Took Her First Steps Into Footwear…" *Footwear News*, December 6, 1999.

Morra, Bernadette. "Handbag Designer Has Plenty of 'Pursonality.'" *Toronto Star*, April 24, 1997.

"The Name of the Game; Brand Building and a Need for Retail Differentiation Make Licensing an Increasingly Viable Option in Home Furnishings." *HFN The Weekly Newspaper for the Home Furnishing Network*, June 7, 2004.

Naughton, Julie. "Kate's New Bag: Carefully Crafted Bag." *Women's Wear Daily*, February 8, 2002.

————. "Kate's New Bag: Acting." *Women's Wear Daily*, April 5, 2002.

————. "Kate Spade on Tour: Bagging the Business." *Women's Wear Daily*, November 1, 2002.

Newby, Leslie. "Kate Spade's New Bag: Home." *HFN The Weekly Newspaper for the Home Furnishing Network*, November 5, 2001.

O'Connor, Anne Marie. "You at Your Best." *Chicago Tribune*, March 24, 1996.

"O'Connor Leaves Spade." *Women's Wear Daily*, November 16, 1998.

Ozzard, Janet. "Kate Spade's Retail Roadshow." *Women's Wear Daily*, November 6, 2000.

Paulson, Kristen. "Kate Spade Comes Home." *Boston Globe,* February 5, 2004.

Peden, Lauren David. "The Inner Lives of Purses." *New York Times*, November 19, 2000.

"Queen of Spades." *Town & Country*, February 2004.

Reed, Julia. "Miss Congeniality: Think of Kate Spade and think of mules, cocktails, cinch waists, and ice cream colors." *Vogue*, August 2004.

Rozhon, Tracie. "Big Deal: Good Bone Structure." *New York Times*, August 19, 1999.

————. Rozhon, Tracie. "Handbag Maker takes Aim at Knockoffs." *New York Times*, October 29, 2002.

————. Rozhon, Tracie. "New Low-Cost Airline Giving Staff a Designer Look." *New York Times.* August 13, 2003.

Ryan, Susan C. "For Designer Kate Spade, Success Is in the Bag." *Boston Globe*, July 14, 1999,

Saeks, Diane Dorrans. "Spade Suits San Francisco: New Accessories Store Caters to Men with Jack Spade Line and a 'Husband Chair.'" *Daily News Record*, December 11, 2000.

Sanders, Lisa. "New Approach for Kate Spade; Narrative Used to Sell Accessories." *Advertising Age*, August 5, 2002.

Santorelli, Dina. "Kate Spade Digs New Line; Inks First U.S. License; Decorative Stationery Items to Complement Handbags." *HFN The Weekly Newspaper for the Home Furnishing Network*, March 2, 1998.

Severs, Heather Bracher. "A Designer's Mother's Day." *Town & Country*, May 2000.

Sheldon, Michael. "Spade Branches Out." *Women's Wear Daily,* July 27, 1998.

Sherman, Lauren. "Spadework." *Forbes*, July 28, 2007.

Sloan, Carole. "Kate's Home Pulls It Together." *Home Textiles Today*, November 3, 2003.

Spade, Kate. *Manners*. New York: Simon & Schuster, 2004.
————. *Occasions*. New York: Simon & Schuster, 2004.

————. *Style*. New York: Simon & Schuster, 2004.

"Spade Fraud Suit Nixed." *Women's Wear Daily*, May 17, 1999.

"Spade's Street Scenes." *Women's Wear Daily*, November 6, 1995.

"Spade Sues DH, Kmart for Knockoffs." *Women's Wear Daily*, January 15, 1997.

"Spade Times Two." *Women's Wear Daily*, September 16, 1996.

Spragins, Ellyn. "Kate and Andy Spade: How We Bagged Our Careers, Pursued Our Passion for Fashion, and Turned a Simple Purse Into a Symbol of Style and a Burgeoning Empire." *Fortune Small Business*, September 1, 2003.

Official Web site of St. Teresa's Academy. http://www.stteresasacademy.org/

Sulcas, Roslyn. "Giants of Design." *House Beautiful,* June 2004.

Tapert, Annette. "Kate's Place: Designer Kate Spade Brings a Dash of her Trademark Whimsy to a Park Avenue Classic." *Town & Country,* October 2004.

Thompson, Clifford, ed. "Kate Spade." Current Biography 68, no. 4 (April 2007): 82-88.

Thompson, Stephanie. "Kate Spade; Andy Spade." *Advertising Age,* November 1, 2004.

————. "Wall to Wall Kate Spade in NYC." *Advertising Age*, September 12, 2005.

Tien, Ellen. "Perambulating Preppy Style." *New York Times*, August 11, 2002.

Tishchler, Linda. "Power Couple." *Fast Company*, March 1, 2005. http://www.fastcompany.com/magazine/92/open_power-couple.html.

Toy, Vivian S. "High-End Leather, Low-End Labor; Handbag Workers Embroiled in Bitter Contract   Dispute." *New York Times*, September 22, 1999.

Tucker, Ross. "NYPD Seizes $2 Million in Counterfeit Goods." *Women's Wear Daily*, September 30, 2005.

Walton, A. Scott. "Style: A Clothing Line Not in Cards for Kate Spade's Empire." *Atlanta Journal-Constitution.* October 26, 2003.

Webb, Carla, and Allison Zisko. "Flatware lines From Vera Wang and Kate Spade Benefit From the Collections' Popularity and Cross-Merchandising Opportunities." *HFN The Weekly Newspaper for the Home Furnishing Network*, September 5, 2005.

Weissman, Katherine B. "Write, She Said." *O, The Oprah Magazine*, September 2006.

Witchel, Alex. "New Kit Bags, to Send Troubles Packing." *New York Times,* December 16, 2001.

White, Constance C. R. "Patterns." *New York Times,* June 6, 1995.

White, Jackie. "For Kate Spade, Success Is in the Bag." *Buffalo News,* December 28, 1997.

———. "Kate Spade Goes Beyond Hand Bags." *Kansas City Star,* April 20, 2000.

———. "Kate Spade: The Woman and the Brand Share a Flexible Nature." *Kansas City Star,* September 10, 2002.

———. "Want to Feel Chic? Designers Share Secrets of Their Favorite New York Haunts." *Kansas City Star,* December 12, 2003.

Wilson, Eric. "Missed Manners." *W,* May 2004.

———. "Baggage Claim." *W,* December 2001.

Wiltz, Teresa. "Off the Cuff." *Chicago Tribune,* September 26, 1996.

Winters, Rebecca. "Kate Spade" (Women in Fashion: The Power List/Trailblazers: Pioneering New Niche Markets). *Time,* February 16, 2004.

Witchel, Alex. "New Kit Bags, to Send Troubles Packing (Kate Spade store in NYC). *New York Times,* December 16, 2001.

Wong, Edward. "Dispute With Handbag Maker Taken to Store." *New York Times,* August 4, 2000.

Zisko, Allison. "An Ace With Spade? Lenox Hopes It Has a Winning Hand With Its New Kate Spade Tabletop Collection." *HFN The Weekly Newspaper for the Home Furnishing Network,* October 27, 2003.

Web Sites

http://www.katespade.com
Kate Spade bags, shoes, accessories, clothing, and more are on display at this site.

http://www.nytimes.com
Nearly thirty articles chronicling the career of Kate Spade are featured on the online edition of the *New York Times.*

Index

Picture Credits

2:	Richard Levine / Alamy
8-9:	Courtesy of Paul Keleher
10-11:	V1 / Alamy
12-13:	Used under license from iStockphoto.com
15:	Allstar Picture Library / Alamy
18-19:	Used under license from iStockphoto.com
20:	AP Photo/Bebeto Matthews
23:	Used under license from iStockphoto.com
24-25:	Used under license from iStockphoto.com
26-27:	Used under license from iStockphoto.com
28-29:	CANDACE BARBOT/MCT /Landov
31:	AP Photo/Kristie Bull/Graylock.com
32-33:	AP Photo/Bebeto Matthews
34-35:	Frances Roberts / Alamy
37:	AP Photo/Tammie Arroyo
40-41:	Kyodo /Landov
44:	ANDREW GOMBERT/Landov
47:	Allstar Picture Library / Alamy
50-51:	Richard Levine / Alamy
56-57:	AP Photo/Ng Han Guan
60-61:	Richard Levine / Alamy
63:	V1 / Alamy
66-67:	AP Photo/Bebeto Matthews
70-71:	Richard Levine / Alamy
73:	Peter J. Hatcher / Alamy
76-77:	JILL JOHNSON/MCT /Landov
79:	LAURA MUELLER/MCT /Landov
82:	AP Photo/Jennifer Graylock
86-87:	Douglas Lander / Alamy
89:	Used under license from iStockphoto.com
92:	JOYCE MARSHALL/MCT /Landov
95:	V1 / Alamy